50 WALKS IN

Snowdonia & North Wales

50 WALKS OF 2–10 MILES

First published 2003
Researched and written by John Gillham
Field checked and updated 2007 by Dennis Kelsall and Jon Sparks

Series Management: Bookwork Creative Associates
Series Editors: Sandy Draper and Marilynne Lanng
Designers: Elizabeth Baldin and Andrew Milne
Picture Research: Lesley Grayson
Proofreaders: Suzanne Juby and Pamela Stagg
Cartography provided by the Mapping Services Department of AA Publishing

Produced by AA Publishing
© Automobile Association Developments Limited 2008

Published by AA Publishing (a trading name of Automobile Association Developments Limited,
whose registered office is Fanum House, Basing View, Basingstoke, Hampshire RG21 4EA;
registered number 1878835)

 This product includes mapping data licensed from the Ordnance
Survey® with the permission of the Controller of Her Majesty's
Stationery Office.
© Crown Copyright 2008. All rights reserved. Licence number 100021153.

A03370

ISBN: 978-0-7495-5599-3

A CIP catalogue record for this book is available from the British Library.

The contents of this book are believed correct at the time of printing. Nevertheless, the
publishers cannot be held responsible for any errors or omissions or for changes in the
details given in this book or for the consequences of any reliance on the information it
provides. This does not affect your statutory rights. We have tried to ensure accuracy in this
book, but things do change and we would be grateful if readers would advise us of any
inaccuracies they may encounter.

We have taken all reasonable steps to ensure that these walks are safe and achievable by
walkers with a realistic level of fitness. However, all outdoor activities involve a degree of risk
and the publishers accept no responsibility for any injuries caused to readers whilst following
these walks. For more advice on walking safely see page 144. The mileage range shown on the
front cover is for guidance only – some walks may be less than or exceed these distances.

Visit AA Publishing's website www.theAA.com/travel

Colour reproduction by Keenes Group, Andover
Printed by Printer Trento Srl, Italy

Acknowledgements
The Automobile Association would like to thank the following photographers, companies and
picture libraries for their assistance in the preparation of this book.

3 AA/S Watkins; 9 AA/W Voysey; 32/33 AA/D Croucher; 54/55 AA/A J Hopkins;
72/73 AA/C Jones; 87 AA/R Newton; 88 AA/D Croucher; 102/103 AA/H Williams;
116/117 AA/D Croucher

Every effort has been made to trace the copyright holders, and we apologise in advance for
any accidental errors. We would be happy to apply the corrections in the following edition of
this publication.

Right: The A4086 Llanberis Pass (Walk 26)

50 WALKS IN

Snowdonia & North Wales

50 WALKS OF 2–10 MILES

Contents

Contents

Rating

Each walk is rated for its relative difficulty compared to the other walks in this book. Walks marked +++ are likely to be shorter and easier with little total ascent. The hardest walks are marked +++

Walking in Safety

For advice and safety tips see page 144.

Locator Map

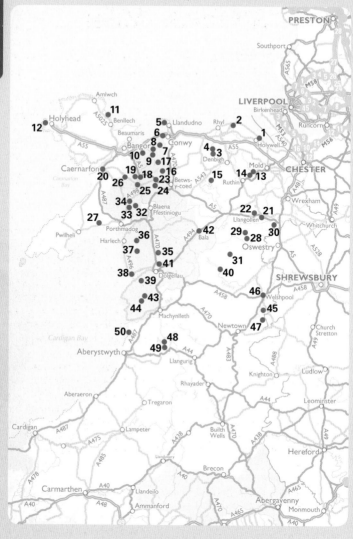

Legend

⇢	Walk Route			Built-up Area
❶	Route Waypoint			Woodland Area
– – –	Adjoining Path	🏻	Toilet
☀	Viewpoint	**P**	Car Park
•	Place of Interest	🖩	Picnic Area
⌂	Steep Section	)(	Bridge

6

Introducing Snowdonia & North Wales

For some, Wales is God's Country. Once you turn your back on the plains of Cheshire and Shropshire, the landscape becomes enticingly hilly, then mountainous. Welsh rivers are boisterous rivers, coursing down from the mountains in white water dashes. Welsh valleys are steep-sided and winding, with secrets around every bend. There are great castles on the coast and great temples of rock in the heartlands of Snowdonia. Having eulogised about it, we should tell you what, for the purposes of this book, the term North Wales means. The 50 Walks series has divided the principality in two, and we have included the northern part of Mid Wales, down to Aberystwyth and Montgomery. In doing so we have encompassed some of the finest wilderness areas as well as the historically fascinating border areas known as the Marches.

Clwyd is the northern gateway to Wales. The old county is green and pleasant, rich farming country with pastures reaching high up hillsides, dotted with whitewashed farmhouses. Valleys like the Tanat and Ceiriog, little known today, have inspired poets for centuries. No one could call Llangollen undiscovered, it's downright busy on most summer weekends, but Llangollen is sited in the midst of north east Wales' finest countryside. The Dee is equally impressive, flowing in great horseshoe meanderings amid the bracken-clad heather hills, the woods and the fields. A walk here can take you up to a hilltop castle, down to an old abbey and ease you along a canal tow path as peaceful as Llangollen is bustling.

The Conwy river separates Clwyd from Snowdonia: the soft greens from the hard grey rock. And the town of Conwy sounds the fanfare for change, with its magnificent town walls and its fairy-tale castle, framed by the great Carneddau mountains. As the walks venture into the Carneddau's expansive area of high whaleback ridges and long uninhabited valleys you will discover the ancient settlements where Iron and Bronze Age tribes lived, and through which Roman soldiers marched. The historical theme continues on the Isle of Anglesey, where it's the coastal walking that appeals.

To the south of the Carneddau, Snowdonia's mountains become even more spectacular with the Glyderau and Snowdon peaks. The Glyderau boast jagged crests with colossal buttresses, the most imposing of these being Tryfan, an almost two-dimensional wedge of rock that towers over Ogwen and its lake.

A book of Welsh walks must include a climb to the highest peak, Snowdon. In this book we have tried to be a bit different, choosing to combine the seldom-trod Eilio ridge for the ascent, with the easy gradients of the popular

PUBLIC TRANSPORT

Like most rural areas, using public transport in North Wales can be problematical, especially on Sundays. The framework is provided by the railway along the north and west coastlines; across Mid Wales between Shrewsbury and Aberystwyth; and from Llandudno Junction to Blanau Ffestiniog. Sherpa buses around Snowdon are very useful, but services become sketchy in the more remote areas. For information call Traveline 0871 200 2233 or visit the website www.traveline-cymru.org.uk.

7

Llanberis path for the descent. It's a long route, but very rewarding. The Snowdonian mountains make a last stand at Cadair Idris, with its ice-scooped corries, arêtes and tarns. If Snowdon is king, then Cadair is crown prince. From the summit you look south to the biscuit-coloured hills of central Wales. Known as the Elenydd or Green Desert, they lack the shape to appeal to the casual walker but for those who take the time to discover them, the Elenydd can be rewarding. You will tread in the footsteps of Owain Glyndwr, come upon little-known waterfalls and crag-strewn mountainsides, and drink from crystal streams. You will have discovered the beating heart of this land of Wales.

Using this book

INFORMATION PANELS

An information panel for each walk shows its relative difficulty (see Walk 5), the distance and total amount of ascent. An indication of the gradients you will encounter is shown by the rating ▲ ▲ ▲ (no steep slopes) to ▲ ▲ ▲ (several very steep slopes).

MAPS

There are 30 maps, covering 40 of the walks. Some walks have a suggested option in the same area. The information panel for these walks will tell you how much extra walking is involved. On short-cut suggestions the panel will tell you the total distance if you set out from the start of the main walk. Where an option returns to the same point on the main walk, just the distance of the loop is given. Where an option leaves the main walk at one point and returns to it at another, then the distance shown is for the whole walk. The minimum time suggested is for reasonably fit walkers and doesn't allow for stops. Each walk has a suggested Ordnance Survey map.

START POINTS

The start of each walk is given as a six-figure grid reference prefixed by two letters indicating which 100-km square of the National Grid it refers to. You'll find more information on grid references on most Ordnance Survey maps.

DOGS

We have tried to give dog owners useful advice about how dog friendly each walk is. Please respect other countryside users. Keep your dog under control, especially around livestock, and obey local bylaws and other dog control notices.

CAR PARKING

Many of the car parks suggested are public, but occasionally you may find you have to park on the roadside or in a lay-by. Please be considerate when you leave your car, ensuring that access roads or gates are not blocked and that other vehicles can pass safely.

Right: Sandbanks in the Afon Mawddach Estuary (Walk 38)

How Grey was my Valley

Follow in the footsteps of monks, martyrs and merchants,
and through more than 1,500 years of history, both
clerical and industrial.

DISTANCE 5 miles (8km)	**MINIMUM TIME** 3hrs
ASCENT/GRADIENT 558ft (170m) ▲▲▲	**LEVEL OF DIFFICULTY** ✛✛✛

PATHS *Woodland paths and tracks, lanes, field paths and coastal embankment, 9 stiles*

LANDSCAPE *Wooded former industrial valley, pastured hillside and coast*

SUGGESTED MAP *OS Explorer 265 Clwydian Range*

START / FINISH *Grid reference: SJ 197775*

DOG FRIENDLINESS *Dogs should be on lead*

PARKING *Just off A548 at Greenfield*

PUBLIC TOILETS *By visitor centre*

A good head of water has served the Greenfield Valley well over the centuries and that water gushes out from a spring high on the limestone hillsides beneath Holywell. Geologists will tell you that this is a natural phenomenon, but romantics tell a different story. They say St Winefride's Well dates back to the 7th century after St Beuno set up a church here. His daughter Winefride taught in the convent and caught the eye of Caradog, the local chieftain. After being spurned by the young nun, the vengeful Caradog drew his sword and cut off her head. Immediately, a spring emerged where her head hit the ground. Since then, pilgrims have been coming to this 'Lourdes of Wales' to take the healing waters. In 1499 Margaret, the Countess of Derby and mother of Henry VII, financed the building of an ornate chapel around the well.

Basingwerk Abbey

The religious connections also played a prominent role in the 12th century, when the Savignac Order, which was later to be combined with the Cistercians, set up Basingwerk Abbey at the bottom of the hill. The abbey is the first thing you see at the start of the walk and, although it has been in ruins since the Dissolution of the Monasteries, a couple of fine sandstone arches remain in good condition.

The Industrial Revolution

The monks were the first to utilise the power of the stream when they built a corn mill here. It would be one of many industrial buildings that would later occupy the whole valley from the mid-17th century onwards. Tall brick chimneys, mill pools, reservoirs and waterwheels sprung up everywhere, and steam from those chimneys billowed up through the trees as the valley was put to work. Thomas Williams of the Parys Mine Company established a rolling mill and the Abbey Wire Mill here, while in the Battery Works up the hill the workforce hammered out brass pots and pans that were used for the slave trade. Ships would leave Liverpool laden with brassware for West Africa, where they would load up with slaves for the Caribbean, returning to Liverpool with sugar, tobacco and cotton. In 1869 the railway came and by 1912 a full passenger service was operating from Greenfield to Holywell. At a gradient of 1 in 27 it became the steepest conventional passenger railway in Great Britain, and continued to be so until its closure in 1954. One by one the mills shut down. Some were demolished, others were left to crumble just like the abbey they surrounded.

Heritage Park

Today the valley is a heritage park and relics of the old industries sit among pleasant gardens. The Greenfield Valley makes a wonderful walk through more than 1,500 years of history and, as you cross the high fields later in this walk, you can see the new century's industries along the coastline of the Dee Estuary far below.

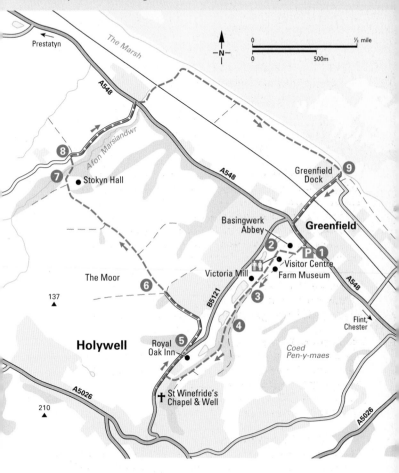

WALK 1 DIRECTIONS

❶ Take the footpath that emerges from the back of the car park on the left-hand side and follow it around the abbey.

❷ Turn left between the visitor centre and the old schoolhouse

on a track that passes Abbey Farm. Take the left fork by the brick walls of Abbey Wire Mill, following the sign to the Fishing Pool, a lily covered pond.

❸ Beyond Victoria Mill take the lower right-hand fork then bear right past some fixed iron gates to pass the crumbling remains of Meadow Mill. Beyond the mill turn left up some steps, climbing up by a weir and back on to the main track.

4 Turn right along the lower track, eventually passing above Hall's soft drinks factory. Beyond a brick chimney, fork off right down to a kissing gate and wind out to the road. Turn left along the road as far as St Winefride's Chapel and Well. When you've viewed these, go back down the road to the Royal Oak Inn.

5 Climb the lane, called Green Bank, that begins from the opposite side of the road. Beyond the houses bear off right along a waymarked track. Keep ahead past the entrance to a small housing estate on a sunken hedged path. Enter a field over a stile at the top.

6 Head out to the distant right corner and continue at the edge of the next field. Maintain your north-westerly direction to a stile and keep going to another, part-way down the boundary. Walk on with a hedge on your right, exiting over a stile onto a track.

7 Leave the cart track where it swings round to the right for a second time and follow a signed footpath across a meadow and then through trees to the banks of

Afon Marsiandwr. After crossing the stream the path climbs out of the woods and crosses a field to reach a country lane.

8 Turn right along the lane following it down to reach the coast road (A548). Cross the busy road with care. The continuing footpath to the seashore lies immediately opposite you, over a step stile. Cross a field and then a railway track, again with care as trains are not infrequent, and continue walking until you get to the inner flood embankments where you turn right.

9 The footpath comes out by Greenfield Dock. Turn right here along the lane back into Greenfield. Turn left to return to the car park.

PRESTATYN

Where the Mountains Meet the Sea

A nature walk through wooded hillsides and limestone knolls with a coastal panorama from Prestatyn to Llandudno's Great Orme.

DISTANCE 3.5 miles (5.6km)   MINIMUM TIME 2hrs

ASCENT/GRADIENT 820ft (250m) ▲▲▲   LEVEL OF DIFFICULTY ✚✚✚

PATHS Well-defined woodland paths and tracks

LANDSCAPE Limestone hillside and mixed woodland

SUGGESTED MAP OS Explorer 264 Vale of Clwyd or 265 Clwydian Range

START / FINISH Grid reference: SJ 071821

DOG FRIENDLINESS Dogs should be on leads

PARKING Picnic site at foot of hill

PUBLIC TOILETS None on route

Just half a mile (800m) back from the golden sands, lively arcades and souvenir shops of Prestatyn there's a hill; a lovely limestone escarpment, enshrouded to its rim with scrub woodland and criss-crossed with shaded footpaths. If you've walked Offa's Dyke you'll know this place as Prestatyn Hillside; it lies at the end of the 182-mile (293km) distance route, and at the end of the Clwydian mountain range. Due to its diverse plant and wildlife the area has been included within the boundaries of the Clwydian Range Area of Outstanding Natural Beauty.

How it Was

If you came to this area a couple of hundred years ago there would have been quite a different scene. Prestatyn's life as a seaside resort had only just begun with the building of the Chester-to-Holyhead railway in 1848. Animal grazing kept the hill slopes as open pastureland, and the underlying limestone rocks had been ravaged by copper and lead mining, and later quarrying. The quarrying ceased in the 1950s with the closure of Manor Hill Works. Slowly, scrub woodland encroached upon the hill, partly concealing the quarry faces and providing new habitats for a diverse range of birds and insects. Stonechats and warblers are a common sight here, choosing to nest in the gorse scrub.

If You Go Down to the Woods Today

Sessile oak is the predominant tree, with hawthorn and sycamore also common. It's very noticeable that the woodland floor and many of the trees are cloaked thickly with ivy. Fortunately for the trees, it's quite harmless to their existence. Bluebells and dog violets add a little colour to the scene, while the less shaded, grassy areas have been colonised by the early purple orchid. In the middle stages of the walk, the path leads to the top edge of the wood with high fields stretching away to the nearby village of Gwaenysgor.

Graig Fawr – a Limestone Gem

Ahead you can see the next objective, Graig Fawr, a little limestone hill once owned by steel magnate, Sir Geoffrey Summers, who donated it to the National Trust. It's a treasure of a hill with places to picnic, either on its lush undulating lawns or its gleaming white rock outcrops. Distant views include most of the North Wales coastline, from the estuary of the Dee to Llandudno's Great Orme, the emerald pastures of the Vale of Clwyd, and the Carneddau mountains, blue and hazy beyond the rolling hills of Denbighshire.

The home run uses the trackbed of an old railway and paths through the shade of Coed yr Esgob (Bishops Wood). Here you'll see limestone-loving trees such as the whitebeam, dogwood and small-leafed lime, interspersed with sessile oaks and sycamores. You'll also see the entrance to an old calcite mine shaft, hidden in the rock face behind the trees.

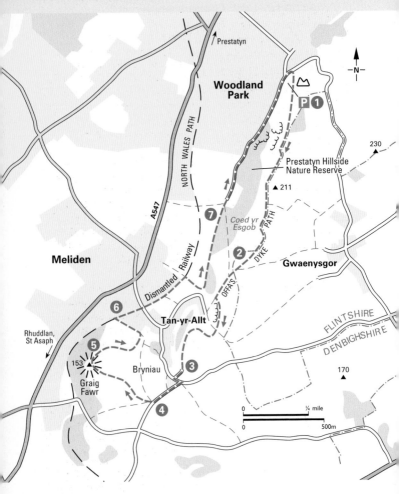

WALK 2 DIRECTIONS

❶ Turn right, out of the car park and climb a few paces up the steep lane. Turn right along the public footpath marked with the Offa's Dyke National Trail acorn sign. This enters an area of scrubby

woodland with a wire fence to the right, before climbing above some quarry workings. As the footpath reaches high fields, ignore all the paths off to the left.

❷ Continue along the top edge of the woods towards Tan-yr-Allt, eventually dropping to a junction. Go left, passing above another quarry and then around a wooded cove. Ignore a path off left there, and later, at a waymark, keep ahead towards Bryniau.

WHERE TO EAT AND DRINK

The Plough Inn at St Asaph is worth the detour. This 18th-century former coaching inn is noted for its real ales and was the winner of the Welsh Seafood Pub of the Year in 2001. It's themed on horse racing, with the Paddock Bar serving lighter meals and the Racecourse Bistro serving seafood dishes, steaks and Welsh lamb. There's also an Italian menu in the Graffiti Italiano restaurant.

③ Go through a kissing gate on to a metalled lane by Red Roofs. Turn left at the next junction, then right a few paces further on, to follow a lane rounding the south side of Graig Fawr.

④ Turn right through a gate on to the Graig Fawr Estate and follow a footpath leading to the trig point on the summit.

WHAT TO LOOK OUT FOR

The early purple orchid is a common sight on Prestatyn Hillside, but it's a delightful plant that flowers between April and June. The purple-pink blooms have three sepals, one forming a hood. Unfortunately, their aroma has been likened to that of a tomcat.

⑤ Descend eastwards along a grassy path that weaves through bracken to pass beneath an overhead power cable at the edge of a wood. Now stepped, the onward way drops beside a fence into the trees, emerging through a kissing gate at the bottom.

⑥ Turn right along a disused railway track, before taking the second footpath on the right, that crosses a field back towards Prestatyn Hillside. Turn left and follow a footpath into Coed yr Esgob, the woods at the foot of Prestatyn Hillside.

⑦ Where the path divides, take the upper fork that joins Bishopwood Lane. Follow this back to a junction near the car park at the start of the walk.

WHILE YOU'RE THERE

Rhuddlan Castle is one of the 'iron ring' castles built for Edward I to subdue the Welsh. Sited by the banks of the Afon Clwyd, the castle has an impressive frontage with a mighty twin-towered gatehouse. It's the only one of Edward's castles to be sited inland, but these early engineers facilitated seaborne access by straightening and widening the 3-mile (5km) course of the Clwyd. The construction required the employment of 1,800 ditchers.

With the Poet to Mynydd y Gaer

Visit an Iron Age fort and look down on the magnificent land- and seascapes that inspired a 19th-century priest and poet.

DISTANCE 3.25 miles (5.2km)	MINIMUM TIME 2hrs
ASCENT/GRADIENT 656ft (200m) ▲▲▲	LEVEL OF DIFFICULTY +++
PATHS *Field paths and tracks, 1 stile*	
LANDSCAPE *Pastured hills*	
SUGGESTED MAP *OS Explorer 264 Vale of Clwyd*	
START / FINISH *Grid reference: SH 981706*	
DOG FRIENDLINESS *Farmland – dogs should be on lead at all times*	
PARKING *Llannefydd village car park*	
PUBLIC TOILETS *At car park*	

'Lovely the woods, waters, meadows, combes, vales,
All the air things wear that build this world of Wales;
Only the inmate does not correspond:
God, lover of souls, swaying considerate scales,
Complete thy creature dear O where it fails,
Being mighty a master, being a father and fond'

Gerard Manley Hopkins

The 19th-century poet and Jesuit priest, Gerard Manley Hopkins (1844–89) loved the borderlands of Clwyd, as can be appreciated from this second verse of his poem, In the Valley of the Elwy. He came to St Beuno's College in the nearby Clwydian Hills in 1874 to study theology. Here he learned the native tongue and applied the rhythms of Welsh poetry to his own religious works, inventing what he described as 'sprung rhythm'. Unfortunately, he was never published in his own lifetime and it was only in 1918, when friend Robert Bridges became Poet Laureate and sent Hopkins' poems to a publisher, that they saw the light of day.

The Village

This short walk will take you from the peaceful little village of Llannefydd and over one of Clwyd's little hills, where you can view the length of Hopkins' Elwy Valley. Llannefydd is 800ft (244m) above sea level and was named after the 5th-century Celtic Saint, Nefydd, who established her church near the spot where the present 13th-century church stands. Before the great engineer Thomas Telford built his A5 trunk road in the 1820s, Llannefydd was on the main route to Holyhead, and the Hawk & Buckle Inn was a stop-off for the stagecoaches. Today Llannefydd is a peaceful backwater and non-the-worse for that – it will be our discovery!

The Fort

Mynydd y Gaer above the village is an Iron Age encampment, probably about 3,000 years old. The ancient earthwork ramparts around its outer edge are well preserved, though today they're covered with scrub and gorse. At the top of the hill there's a more modern cairn – a pile of stones with a pole in the middle.

MYNYDD Y GAER

From here you can see why those early settlers chose this place – they could see for miles across the land and out to sea! Below and to the north you can view Gerard Manley Hopkins' beloved Afon Elwy, twisting and turning between low wooded hills. It meanders into the beautiful flatlands of the Vale of Clwyd before finally flowing into the sea at Rhyl, whose tall white tower can be easily picked out against the bay. On either side you can see a mountain range. To the east the heathered Clwydians, which decline to the sea at Prestatyn, and to the west are the distinctive Snowdonian peaks, from the Carneddau whalebacks in the north to Snowdon itself.

Eyecatching Light

Strangely enough, if the sun shines it may well be a little reservoir, Plâs-uchaf, that catches your eye. Beautifully set tucked beneath Mynydd y Gaer's west slopes, its surrounding velvety pastures, complete with whitewashed farmhouse, make it stand out as an idyllic retreat. You get a closer look on the way back on a lovely green track that skirts the foot of the hill and its northern shores.

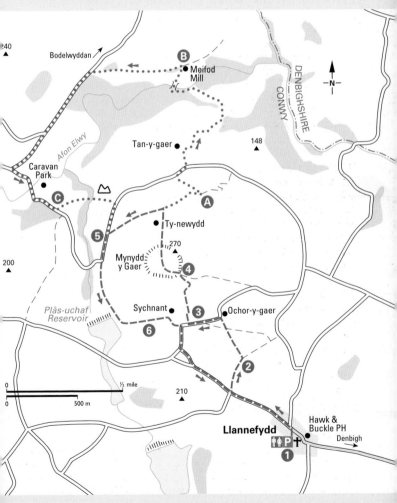

WALK 3 DIRECTIONS

WALK 3

1 Turn left out of the car park and follow the lane signposted to Llanfair TH (the TH standing for Talhaiarn). Where a road comes in from the left, go though a gate on the right-hand side and traverse the fields with a hedge and fence on your left.

2 Beyond a gate in the far corner, turn left with the hedge, continuing uphill in a second field and then over a stile. Leave through a gate at the top, winding out of a small enclosure onto a lane by Ochor-y-gaer. Turn left.

> ### WHERE TO EAT AND DRINK
> The Hawk & Buckle Inn, a 17th-century coaching inn, is well known for its fine cuisine and welcoming ambience, including open fires and black roof beams. Ashley Courteney has recommended the restaurant, which uses only fresh ingredients, including local lamb, beef and salmon. For those wanting a more informal meal, the bar has an extensive menu including vegetarian food.

3 Where the road turns sharply to the left, leave it and double-back to the right on a tarmac track climbing up to Bryn Hwylfa. Just past the whitewashed cottage, turn left along an enclosed grass track climbing the hill. Beyond a gate a grassy footpath winds through gorse and scrub before

veering left beneath the outer ring defences of the Iron Age fort.

4 Where the gorse bushes become more sparse, climb right to reach the brow of the hill. Go through a farm gate to reach the cairn at the summit. Descend north from here, to pick up a track that passes a hilltop farm, Ty-newydd, before descending left to meet another lane.

5 Turn left along the lane, but leave it at a right-hand bend for a grass track continuing ahead to pass above the shores of Plâs-uchaf Reservoir. Past the lake, the track swings left towards Sychnant.

6 Beyond a gate the track becomes a path, winding through woodland before coming to the lane that you left on your outward route. Turn right along the lane then first left, heading straight back to Llannefydd.

> ### WHAT TO LOOK OUT FOR
> The thickets around the fort have honeysuckle and dog rose growing in them, but the main plant is gorse, whose golden yellow blooms can emblazon the hillsides as early as January. If you hear a sound like two pebbles being tapped together it will almost certainly be the tiny stonechat, a tawny breasted bird with distinctive white streaks on its neck. It can often be seen perched on the gorse bushes, nervously flicking its tail and wings.

> ### WHILE YOU'RE THERE
> Bodelwyddan on the edge of Clwyd's coastal plains, not far from Llannefydd, has a church and a castle that are worth seeing. The castle is now an outpost of the National Portrait Gallery and is open most days of the year. Set in 260 acres (105ha) of formal gardens and woodland, the 19th-century castle is sumptuously furnished. There are walks and nature trails around the grounds. The church has a 200ft (61m) spire, constructed out of gleaming white limestone and marble.

In the Elwy Valley

In the sylvan river valley immortalised by Gerard Manley Hopkins.
See map and information panel for Walk 3

WALK

4

DISTANCE *5.5 miles (8.8km)*   MINIMUM TIME *3hrs 30min*
ASCENT/GRADIENT *1,197ft (365m)* ▲▲▲   LEVEL OF DIFFICULTY ✦✦✦

WALK 4 DIRECTIONS
(Walk 3 option)

When you're looking down from the summit of Mynydd y Gaer, you cannot help being enticed towards the luscious green valley of the Elwy. Its pretty woodland and cow pastures could have been plucked from a Gainsborough masterpiece. So let's go and see for ourselves.

From the top of Mynydd y Gaer, descend to the same track as in Point ❹, but this time, just past the farm of Ty-newydd, leave the main track for a grassy one heading right. Approaching a gate, swing left to pass beneath old cottages (Point ❹), before making a zig-zagging descent to a narrow, gated lane that runs along the north side of the hill.

Turn right along the lane, then left along an enclosed grassy track. On reaching Tan-y-gaer, a pretty whitewashed farm, double-back right on a waymarked and winding sunken track that can be muddy after wet weather and, for a short stretch, overgrown in summer.

The track ends in a field beneath a steep bank on the left. Here, go through the left of two gates, then head left (west-north-west) across the field and towards the river (trackless). At the riverbank go through a gate on your left to follow a path through the woods.

Come to and cross a substantial footbridge over the Elwy before walking across a field towards the whitewashed Meifod Mill, Point ❸. Just before the gate, turn left through trees on a raised path that follows the course of the old mill leat. After going through a gate, the path climbs to the right and over a stile, out into high fields. Go left, crossing an intervening stile and aiming for the far top corner of a second field. Through a gate, continue by the left boundary to emerge over a stile on to a lane.

Turn left along the road and take two left forks to descend to a one-arched stone bridge that takes you back over the Elwy. Continue along the lane, past a caravan park before climbing past woodland. Ignore the first gate on the left, but go through the second, Point ❷. Walk forward to a rutted track and drop left through a fence. Follow it right, a path developing at the far end that descends to a stream. Cross and climb steeply away up the hillside to the road beneath Mynydd y Gaer. Turn right to join Walk 3 at Point ❺.

Alice's Wonderland

The Great Orme is a fascinating world of limestone sea cliffs.

DISTANCE *5 miles (8km)*	MINIMUM TIME *3hrs*
ASCENT/GRADIENT *1,033ft (314m)* ▲▲▲	LEVEL OF DIFFICULTY +✛✛

NOTE *(fairly easy after steep, initial climb)*

PATHS *Well-defined paths and tracks*

LANDSCAPE *Grassland and limestone cliffs and bluffs*

SUGGESTED MAP *OS Explorer OL17 Snowdon*

START / FINISH *Grid reference: SH 781827*

DOG FRIENDLINESS *Dogs will love this walk but keep on lead around Parc Farm*

PARKING *Town car parks or take road to summit pay car park*

PUBLIC TOILETS *At Llandudno's main car park and at summit*

WALK 5 DIRECTIONS

It has been said that Lewis Carroll was inspired to write *Alice's Adventures in Wonderland* after a visit to Llandudno and, after seeing the caves, rabbit warrens and captivating scenery of the quieter corners, you can see why. In summer, however, the Great Orme is teeming with visitors who come by car, by Victorian tramcars, and by chairlift. But there's another side to the Great Orme. It has been designated a Site of Special Scientific Interest (SSSI), for this is a limestone promontory with diverse vegetation, ranging from marine grassland to acid heath. There's

WHERE TO EAT AND DRINK

There's a café and the bustling Randolph Turpin Bar on the summit of the Great Orme. For a good pub meal try The Queen's Head at Llandudno Junction. They use fresh local produce like Conwy salmon and local Welsh beef alongside game and vegetarian dishes.

history around every corner, with Europe's only Bronze Age copper mines that are open to the public; an Iron Age fort, caves inhabited in the upper Palaeolithic period, and St Tudno's Church, with origins in the 6th century.

You could start from the summit car park, but that would be cheating, so the route description begins from Llandudno Pier. Walk along the Marine Drive and bear left to the Happy Valley Gardens before following the waymarks for the Great Orme summit, along a zig-zag surfaced path on the right that climbs through the park. At the top of the parkland go through a gate and follow the path above a little limestone ravine that has now been filled by a dry-ski slope and toboggan run. There's a pleasant Swiss-style café in the complex for those who have already worked up an appetite.

Having lost its tarmac, the path continues uphill beneath outcropping limestone on to high grassy slopes. If you detour off the

WHILE YOU'RE THERE

Visit the Alice in Wonderland Centre in Trinity Square, Llandudno. Alice Liddell, the real Alice, had a house on the West Shore. You can walk through the rabbit hole, see life-size displays and hear story excerpts.

path a few paces up the hill you'll see a great view across the pier and Llandudno Bay, to the town and beaches, which yawn out to a second limestone promontory, known as the Little Orme.

On the Great Orme's marine grasslands many of the well-known limestone species are present – wild thyme, bloody cranesbill, common and hoary rock roses and the pretty sky blue spring squill.

Further uphill and inland, the path divides into three. Take the middle one, signposted for the summit. It comes out by the tramway's Halfway Station. Turn right here, following a grassy path on the nearside of the tramway. After crossing St Tudno's road, the path climbs to the summit complex.

The white building with a tower and verandas has a chequered past. Built as a hotel with an 18-hole golf course, it has had many owners and suffered a big fire. The RAF used it as a radar station during World War Two, then champion middleweight boxer Randolph Turpin became licensee. He suffered financial difficulties and in 1966 committed suicide. The golf course has gone now, but there is still a Randolph Turpin Bar. The visitor centre next door is open between Easter and October.

Go round the north side of the summit complex to the cable

car station where a waymarked footpath descends the grassy hillside above St Tudno's Church and graveyard. Turn left along a gravel track and follow it beside the wall surrounding Parc Farm.

Past the rocks known as Free Trade Loaf, the path turns left, still following the wall. Note the limestone pavements here and the plants in the grikes, or cracks. The pink flowered one is called herb Robert. Some grikes contain tiny thorn bushes, dwarfed even by domestic gooseberry bushes.

Turn left again at a cairn. You have now rounded the Orme on to the south side. It's worth a detour from the wall to see the cliff edge and the view across to Conwy Bay, backed by the great Carneddau. The cliffs are colonised by many gulls, including fulmars, kittiwakes, guillemots and razorbills.

When the little cliff path runs out, return to the wall and follow it high above the cliffs to a corner. Ignore the well-used path going left for the summit complex, instead take the path bearing half left. Turn right on meeting the summit road. On reaching the Copper Mines and the Halfway Station, either retrace your steps across the high fields, back through Happy Valley (the pretty way) or continue along the road by the side of the tramway into Llandudno (the short way).

WHAT TO LOOK OUT FOR

In the heathland you can see both ling, the most commonly seen moorland heather, and bell heather, which has a brighter, larger flower. Scattered among it you will see dwarf and common gorse and pungent-smelling juniper.

Conwy: Castle High and Castle Low

Conwy's magnificent castle lies at the foot of the Carneddau, but up there in the foothills there's a fort, an outpost of the Celtic era.

DISTANCE 6.75 miles (10.9km)	MINIMUM TIME 4hrs

ASCENT/GRADIENT 1,493ft (455m) ▲▲▲ LEVEL OF DIFFICULTY ✦✦✦

PATHS Good paths and easy-to-follow moorland tracks, 5 stiles

LANDSCAPE Town, coastline high ridge, farmland and copse

SUGGESTED MAP OS Explorer OL17 Snowdon

START / FINISH Grid reference: SH 783775

DOG FRIENDLINESS OK on high ridges, but keep on lead elsewhere

PARKING Large car park on Llanrwst Road behind Conwy Castle

PUBLIC TOILETS At car park

Conwy is special. Approaching from Llandudno Junction, three fine bridges (including Thomas Telford's magnificent suspension bridge of 1822) cross the estuary beneath the mighty castle, allowing the road and the railway into this medieval World Heritage Site. The fortress dates back to 1287, when the powerful English King Edward I built it as part of his 'iron ring' to repress the rebellious troops of Llewelyn the Great, who had given him a great deal of trouble in his conquest of Wales.

Great town walls with gates and towers still encircle old Conwy. You should walk these walls, for they offer a fine rooftop view of the castle, the Conwy Estuary and the rocky knolls of Deganwy, before you arrive at the quayside where you can watch the fishermen sorting their nets and the seagulls watching out for any scraps. The walk description begins at the quayside, not the car park, as you will probably want to take a good look around this medieval town. The route starts on a shoreline path under the boughs of Bodlondeb Wood.

The Ancient Settlements of Conwy Mountain

Not long after passing through Conwy's suburbs you're walking the hillside, on a path threading through gorse and small wind-twisted hawthorns. If you liked the views from the castle walls, you'll love the view from the Conwy Mountain ridge. Looking back you can see the castle, towering over the town's roof tops; but now added to the scene are the Carneddau, the limestone isthmus of the Great Orme and, across the great sands of Lafan, Anglesey.

There is quite a network of paths criss-crossing the ridge and usually the best course is the highest: you'll need to be on the crest path to see the remains of Castell Caer. This 10-acre (4ha) fort has been linked to both Roman and Iron-Age settlers – it certainly has formidable defences, with clearly visible artificial ramparts that overlook spectacular sea cliffs on one side, and a wide view of the land to the south. Beyond the fort, the path misses out the peaks of Penmaen-bach and Alltwen, which is just as well, for the former has been heavily quarried for its roadstone – you probably drove over some of it on your way up the motorway. Instead you should descend to the Sychnant Pass, a splendid, twisting gorge that separates Conwy Mountain from the higher Carneddau peaks.

CONWY

It's all downhill from here, but the scenery becomes more varied and still maintains interest. As you descend you can see the tidal River Conwy, twisting amongst chequered green fields. Little hills present themselves to you, on your way back north. One last one has pleasant woods with primroses and bluebells, and it gives you another fine view of Conwy Castle to add to your collection before returning to base.

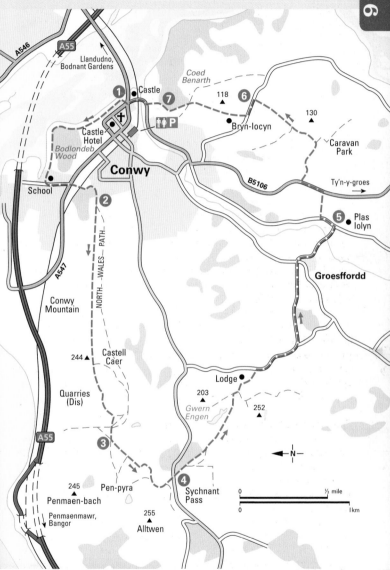

WALK 6 DIRECTIONS

❶ From Conwy Quay head north-west along the waterfront, past the Smallest House and

under the town walls. Fork right along a tarmac waterside footpath that rounds Bodlondeb Wood. Turn left along the road, past the school and on to the A547. Cross

23

WHAT TO LOOK OUT FOR

There is evidence of over 50 Iron-Age hut circles at the Caer Lleion fort on Conwy Mountain. Although the foundations still remain the huts would have been wooden with roofs thatched with rushes and reeds. The Celtic tribes that inhabited the huts would have disappeared from the hills after long battles with the Romans in the first century AD.

the woods on your left. Over a stile carry on past Gwern Engen to meet a track. Go right and then bear left, dropping above the Lodge to reach a lane. Turn right along the lane, then turn left, when you reach the next junction, into Groesffordd village. Cross the road, then take the road ahead that swings to the right past a telephone box, then left (south east) towards Plas Iolyn.

WHERE TO EAT AND DRINK

The Castle Hotel in Conwy's High Street is a rather grand 16th-century hotel that has a brasserie type restaurant and a lively bar where you can get excellent meals if you get there early enough to grab a table.

the road, then the railway line by a footbridge. The track beyond skirts a wood to reach a lane, where you turn right.

2 At a fork bear right past a house to a waymarked stile, from which a footpath rakes up wooded hillsides up on to Conwy Mountain. Follow the undulating crest of Conwy Mountain and continue past Castell Caer.

3 Several tracks converge in the high fields of Pen-Pyra. Here, follow signposts for the North Wales Path along the track heading to the south-west over the left shoulder of Alltwen and down to the metalled road traversing the Sychnant Pass.

4 Follow the footpath from the other side of the road, skirting

WHILE YOU'RE THERE

Bodnant Gardens near Conwy is an 80-acre (32ha) garden of exotic plants, fine herbaceous borders, and ponds with a profusion of water lilies. It is in two parts, the upper known as the Terrace Gardens, is more formal with lawns and borders, while the lower, known as the Dell, has a more natural beauty and includes the Pinetum and Wild Gardens. Open mid-March to late October. Dogs are not allowed in the gardens.

5 Turn left at the end but then leave opposite a white house on a path climbing to a cottage. Cross a track and continue upfield to the B5106. Go left to Conwy Touring Park. Follow the drive to a hairpin, from which a waymarked path climbs through trees, recrossing the drive. Finally emerging through a kissing gate, continue up the field edge. Swing left along an undulating ridge above successive pastures, finally meeting a lane.

6 Turn left, shortly leaving right along a track past a communications mast to Bryn-locyn. Continue at the edge of fields beyond to a stile by Coed Benarth, from which a path drops beside the wood.

7 Go over a ladder stile on your left-hand side and descend a field to a roadside gate at the bottom. Turn right on to the B5106 to return to the quayside, or turn left to get back to the main car park.

Stones and Settlements on Tal y Fan

Visit the most northerly 2,000ft (610m) hill in Wales and see what remains from ancient settlers.

DISTANCE 5 miles (8km)   MINIMUM TIME 3hrs

ASCENT/GRADIENT 984ft (300m) ▲▲▲ LEVEL OF DIFFICULTY +++

PATHS Cart tracks and narrow mountain paths, 7 stiles

LANDSCAPE Moor and mountain

SUGGESTED MAP OS Explorer OL17 Snowdon

START / FINISH Grid reference: SH 720715

DOG FRIENDLINESS Can be off lead on high ridges, but should be kept under tight control in farmland

PARKING Car park at end of Bwlch y Ddeufaen road, off B5106 Conwy–Llanwrst road

PUBLIC TOILETS None en route

When you're driving along the A55 past Colwyn Bay, the first close-up views of Snowdonia reveal themselves across the Conwy Estuary. The peak that captures the eye here rises up behind Conwy Mountain and has just enough crags on top to ruffle its otherwise smooth whaleback outline. The mountain is Tal y Fan, an outlier of the Carneddau range, and the most northerly 2,000-footer (610m) in Wales.

Now you can be a hero and climb Tal y Fan from sea level, but there's a peak-baggers' route that begins from Bwlch y Ddeufaen 1,400ft (427m) up in the hills above the Conwy Valley. From here you can get the wonderful views of Snowdonia and the North Wales coastline, from Anglesey to Conwy and its castle without the toil of a full day's walk.

The Wild Pass

The road you walk is centuries old. Bronze and Iron Age tribesmen would have used it regularly, for they had large settlements all over the northern Carneddau. Great monoliths either side of the road give the pass, Bwlch y Ddeufaen (pass of the two stones) its name.

The Bronze Age Hill Settlers and the Romans

When you climb to the top of Tal y Fan you can see their settlements in plan, for here on a great high plateau the Ordovices tribesmen could farm and watch out for their enemies from over the seas. The Roman invasion under Gnaeus Julius Agricola must have come as a shock to these primitive farmers. Between AD 75 and AD 77 the invaders set up forts at Segontium (Caernarfon) and Canovium (at Caerhun in the Conwy Valley). When the Roman cohorts marched into the hills they made the Bwlch y Ddeufaen road their own, undertaking improvements by surfacing it and adding mileposts. The Ordovices were defeated. Great forts like Caer Bach, on the southern slopes of Tal y Fan, were abandoned. Today, Caer Bach lies beneath the turf and gorse, but with its earth ramparts and a circle of stones still visible. As you look down into the civilisation of the Conwy Valley you can drift back into time and those heartbreaking battles with the superior power.

25

Decline and Fall

As the Roman Empire declined, the native tribes returned to Tal y Fan, tending sheep on the high northern plateau and growing crops on the steeper southern flanks. Looking down to the castle at Conwy you are reminded that although it would be Edward I of England who would come to conquer, it would take the land clearance and enclosure acts of the early 19th century to force the Welsh hill people away from their settlements.

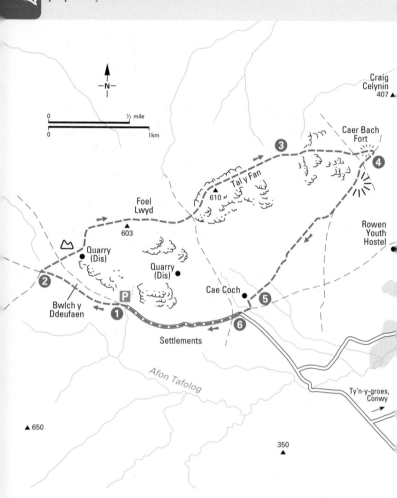

WALK 7 DIRECTIONS

❶ From the car park at the top of the metalled section of the road to Bwlch y Ddeufaen, continue along the road, which is now unsurfaced, and follow it past the ancient standing stones to the high pass itself, where you go through a gate in a crossing wall.

❷ Turn right and follow the course of the wall, across the pass under three lines of electricity pylons, and then up the steep rocky slopes of Foel Lwyd. A narrow footpath continues, first descending to a little saddle, or col, then climbing to the even rockier summit of Tal y Fan.

3 The descending footpath still follows the line of the drystone wall, but stays with more even ground on the left. When the wall turns right, continue straight ahead, towards the prominent hill of Craig Celynin. Thread between outcrops to reach a little green valley running down to the right, where you look for the gorse-covered mound of Caer Bach Fort.

WHERE TO EAT AND DRINK

The Groes Inn at Ty'n-y-groes (B5106 to Conwy) was the first house in Wales to be licensed (1573). It's a splendid old coaching house with low oak-beamed ceilings and roaring fires. The restaurant is known for its fine cuisine. Expect to see game, Welsh lamb, Conwy crab and cured hams on the menu and a blackboard full of specials for those taking a bar meal.

WHAT TO LOOK OUT FOR

You should be able to pick out the field systems of the Bronze Age farmers below the road in the valley of the Tafolog and in the pastures to the north of the youth hostel. Their houses were made of wood but you can still see many of the raised earth platforms they stood on, especially from the track beyond Caer Bach.

5 The footpath becomes a cart track, which passes beneath the whitewashed cottage of Cae Coch before turning left to join the stony vehicle track that has come from Rowen Youth Hostel.

6 Turn right along the track, which soon joins the Bwlch y Ddeufaen road at a sharp corner. Go straight ahead along the road and follow it back to the car park.

4 When you reach the remains of the fort turn right to follow a tumbled down wall heading south-west across high pastureland overlooking the Conwy Valley. Except for a short stretch this wall now acts as your guide, as do the frequent ladder stiles and locked gates sited in all the intervening cross-walls on the route.

WHILE YOU'RE THERE

Plas Mawr in Conwy's High Street claims to be the finest surviving Elizabethan gentry town house in Britain and it's certainly an impressive building. It was built for Robert Gwydir, an influential merchant in the town, between 1576 and 1585. The lime-washed walls and opulent furnishings must have been breathtaking at the time. The house is open from late March to late October.

Pass of the Two Stones

A walk through one of the prettiest woods in Wales,
to a high mountain pass.

DISTANCE *5 miles (8km)* **MINIMUM TIME** *3hrs*

ASCENT/GRADIENT *1,214ft (370m)* ▲▲▲ **LEVEL OF DIFFICULTY** +++

PATHS *Woodland, field and moorland paths, cart tracks, 5 stiles*

LANDSCAPE *Woodland, high pasture and moorland*

SUGGESTED MAP *OS Explorer OL17 Snowdon*

START / FINISH *Grid reference: SH 694739*

DOG FRIENDLINESS *Dogs should be on lead, except on high ridges*

PARKING *Small car park on Newry Drive, Nant-y-pandy, Llanfairfechan*

PUBLIC TOILETS *None en route*

Most people speed by on the A55 dual carriageway without giving Llanfairfechan a second thought or glance. The little Victorian seaside resort beneath the quarry-carved mountain of Penmaenmawr has been forsaken for the castles of Caernarfon and the coastline of Anglesey. Yet Llanfairfechan has a secret valley, a beautiful avenue to the big Carneddau mountains.

Nant-y-Coed is that valley and Llanfair's early visitors knew it well. In the 1900s it was part of the Newry Estate owned by a Mr Massey. Massey leased the valley to local businessman John Rowland Jones who charged visitors for entry. In 1924, after the sale of the estate, the local council purchased Nant-y-Coed to maintain it for recreational purposes.

A tourist poster described Nant-y-Coed as 'the loveliest sylvan rock and river scenery in Wales', and so it is today. A little path, shaded by deciduous woodland of alder, ash, oak and sycamore, is flanked by the Afon Llanfairfechan, which tumbles over mossy rocks. If the sun's shining, its rays will flicker through the canopy and play games with the water, as will the dipper, who can often be seen scudding across the surface before diving in headlong in search of an insect or two. The bouldery river banks are lined with ferns and wild flowers. In spring the bluebell and wild garlic are predominant, but look out for the star-like white blooms of the wood anemone, also the wood sorrel, a low creeping plant with delicate five-petalled white flowers tinged with lilac.

On to the Moors

As you leave the woods behind and enter what the Welsh called Ffridd, you can see why conservationist John Muir referred to sheep as woolly locusts, for the plant life has been severely diminished by their grazing. Few flowers, except the little yellow tormentil, remain. As you gain height, gorse and bracken have infested much of the pasture, while the odd rowan survives, with wind-warped boughs.

By the time you're at the pass Bwlch y Ddeufaen (pass of the two stones) you're into typical Carneddau moor, where sphagnum moss, cotton grass and rushes fill the marshy areas and heather and bilberry cloak the drier rockier areas. It's a more sombre world, one where the quarrelling ravens and buzzards have replaced the colourful little redstarts and pied flycatchers of the woodland.

NANT-Y-COED

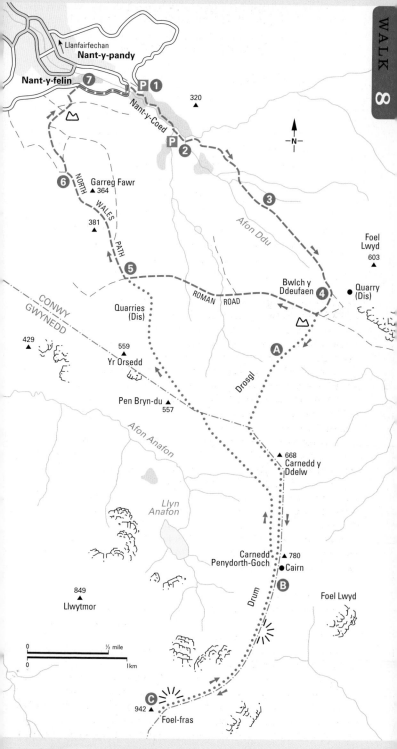

After following the Roman road along these high moors the route returns to that other world, down the side of Garreg Fawr, where you can see the coastal sands and the Isle of Anglesey, and still further into that sylvan river valley.

WALK 8

WALK 8 DIRECTIONS

1 Go through the gate beyond the car park and follow the stony path through the woods of Nant-y-Coed by the stream. Take the more prominent left fork up past the pond, then cross the stream using stepping stones. More stepping stones are used to cross a side stream before climbing to a second car park.

2 A signpost points the way up the valley and you cross a footbridge by a ford to continue. Keep a sharp eye open for stone waymarks, which guide you through a complex series of criss-crossing tracks.

3 The path enters open moorland, still with occasional slate waymarks. Finally, ignore a waymark that points right where the track continues straight ahead. When the path degenerates the direct line is close to steeper rocky slopes on the left. Aim for the col between Foel Lwyd and Drosgl, a point where three lines of pylons straddle the fells.

4 At Bwlch y Ddeufaen a faint path arcs right, parallel to the wall, to join the Roman road. Turn right along the track.

5 At a crossroads of tracks, turn right along the one signposted 'Llanfairfechan' joining the waymarked course of the North Wales Path over Garreg Fawr. After the first grassy summit the path veers left to rake down the west side of the hill to a wall.

6 Take the waymarked right-hand fork rather than the track following the wall down left. Ignore a narrow path forking right. The main track then threads right and descends steeply through pastures overlooking Nant-y-Coed. Turn left down a little enclosed ginnel to the road.

7 Turn right along the road, which rises then descends to a bridge over the Afon Llanfairfechan. At the other side take the narrow lane back to the car park.

Foel-fras

A fair weather climb to Wales' most northerly 3,000ft (914m) summit.

See map and information panel for Walk 8

| DISTANCE 8.75 miles (14.1km) MINIMUM TIME 5hrs 30min |
| ASCENT/GRADIENT 2,950ft (900m) ▲▲▲ LEVEL OF DIFFICULTY ✦✦✦ |

WALK 9 DIRECTIONS
(Walk 8 option)

More people get lost on the Carneddau than any other Welsh mountain range. Though they offer some of the best ridge walking in Britain, they're also notorious for hill fog and mile upon mile of featureless ridge. Choose a settled and sunny summer day and the Carneddau will reward you with a memorable walk on the hills and far reaching views across the Irish Sea and to England's north-west. This route is safer than most, with walls and fences to guide you.

At Bwlch y Ddeufaen, ignore the Roman road, and instead climb the steep wall-side path up the grassy spur of Drosgl, Point Ⓐ. On reaching this first summit, the Anafon Valley comes into view, with stony Llwytmor rearing up beyond the little Anafon reservoir.

The ridge path continues by a fence to Carnedd y Ddelw (cairn of the idol). This summit has something you'll have seen on other Carneddau walks – a Bronze Age burial ground. But Drum (pronounced drim, 'ridge') beckons, and the path continues south towards its summit to join a wide, stony track to the top.

Drum's summit, Point Ⓑ, is called Carnedd Penydorth-Goch and has even better preserved remains of a Bronze Age circular platform. Looking east beyond the neighbouring hill of Pen y Castell you can just make out the concentric rings of a hill fort, Pen-y-Gaer, on one of the lower hills overlooking the Conwy Valley.

Continue south on a peaty path that follows the fence to Foel-fras, Point Ⓒ, the most northerly of the Welsh 3,000ft (914m) summits. Now you can see the major Carneddau peaks; Carnedd Llewelyn (named after the first Prince of Wales), Pen yr Helgi Du (hill of the black hound) and Pen Llithrig y Wrach (slippery hill of the witch). Looking back, Llyn Anafon is set in a twisting valley that leads the eye out to the coast, Puffin Island and Anglesey.

Return to Drum before descending along a track traversing the high slopes on the west side at first then, beyond Carnedd y Ddelw, the eastern slopes. The track meets the crosspaths, Point ❺, and follows Walk 8 back to Nant-y-Coed.

Aber's Twin Falls

See two impressive waterfalls, each tumbling down dark vegetated cliffs.

WALK 10

DISTANCE 4 miles (6.4km) **MINIMUM TIME** 2hrs 30min

ASCENT/GRADIENT 1,050ft (320m) ▲▲▲ **LEVEL OF DIFFICULTY** ✦✦✦

PATHS *Well-defined paths and farm tracks, 8 stiles*

LANDSCAPE *Wild glen, pastured hill slopes, mixed woodland and scree*

SUGGESTED MAP *OS Explorer OL17 Snowdon*

START/FINISH *Grid reference: SH 662720*

DOG FRIENDLINESS *Farmland, dogs should be on lead*

PARKING *Pay car parks either side of bridge*

PUBLIC TOILETS *At main Forest Enterprise pay car park*

WALK 10 DIRECTIONS

Abergwyngregyn village lies on a narrow grassy plain, where the high Carneddau come down to the sea. 'Aber' also lies at the foot of a delightful valley now part of the Coedydd Aber National Nature Reserve, set up in 1975 by the Nature Conservancy Council (now Countryside Council for Wales) as an example of a broadleaved woodland habitat. The Romans arrived here, and built a road from Canovium, their fort near Conwy, to Gorddinog near Aber itself, while on the wooded hillside above the village rooftops, there's an Iron Age fort, Maes y Gaer.

At the back of some village houses is a mound, part of an 11th-century motte-and-bailey castle. It is likely that this was also the site of the palace where Llewelyn the Great, Prince of Wales, held court here in the 13th century. Llewelyn cemented his relationship with the English Crown by marrying Joan the daughter of his old enemy, King John, but the marriage ended in disaster when she had an affair with William de Breos the Younger, Lord of Brycheiniog. Llewelyn had his wife imprisoned and de Breos hanged. Just to the north of the village, Gwern y Grogfa, which means bog of the gallows, is a dark reminder.

Go through the gate at the south end of the lower car park and follow the path through woodland. The path crosses the Afon Rhaeadr-fawr on a footbridge. Through a gate on the other side, turn right to follow a track south through pastures. On your left are dark, commercial spruce woods but in the more swampy ground to the right you'll see alders. In spring the scene will be coloured

WHERE TO EAT AND DRINK

At the Falls Tavern and Restaurant you can have sandwiches and light meals in the bar. Three-course dinners in the Conservatory restaurant might include sirloin steak, lemon sole, stuffed salmon roast or Cajun chicken.

ABER FALLS

with the buttercup like flowers of the marsh marigold.

After passing under rows of pylons you come upon the visitor centre, which is housed in the old farmstead of Nant Rhaeadr (marked Nant on the maps). The centre is well worth seeing. It illustrates how the valley has developed. It tells of a past when the woods were coppiced and harvested for their hardwoods, which were used for railway sleepers and clog making.

Beyond Nant the path climbs steadily through the valley with the top of the Aber Falls clearly visible ahead. The woodlands have thinned out though there are patches of oak wood and mountain ash.

The path leads right to the base of the falls, where the thunderous river plummets hundreds of feet down cliffs of quartz-streaked Cambrian granophyre. The longest single drop is 115ft (35m). Scrub birch trees eke out an existence high on the rock ledges, as do liverworts, rare mosses and lichens, primroses and anemones.

Cross a bridge just below the falls and climb a rocky knoll overlooking the pool. To the right is a ladder stile in the wall (marked 'North Wales Path only: no short return to Aber'). The path heads beneath the cliffs to pass beneath Rhaeadr-bach (the small waterfalls). Now it swings north to traverse the western slopes of the valley and becomes a track on the slopes of Cae'r Mynydd. Watch for a waymark directing you right at a fork, and continue beneath pylons and then below a conifer plantation.

Now the North Wales and Anglesey coasts come into view, with the sands of Traeth Lafan stretching nearly all the way to Anglesey. Before the construction of the Menai Bridge, travellers to and from Anglesey would, at low tide, make their way across the sands to a boat which would take them across the narrow channel near Beaumaris.

The track later drops past derelict stock sheds to a gate and stile. Keep right as it splits, descending below more trees before turning into the plantation. Leave at that point on a steeply falling path towards Abergwyngregyn. Reaching the lane, turn right to return to the car park.

Moelfre and the Ancient Village

Walk along Anglesey's beautiful east coast and discover a remarkably intact ancient village.

DISTANCE	5 miles (8km) MINIMUM TIME 3hrs
ASCENT/GRADIENT	541ft (165m) ▲▲▲ LEVEL OF DIFFICULTY ✦✦✦
PATHS	Well-defined coastal and field paths, 5 stiles
LANDSCAPE	Sea cliffs and coastal pasture
SUGGESTED MAP	OS Explorer 263 Anglesey East
START / FINISH	Grid reference: SH 511862
DOG FRIENDLINESS	Can be off lead on coastal path
PARKING	Car park at entrance to village
PUBLIC TOILETS	In car park and by harbour

Being in Moelfre is like being in Cornwall. The pebble beach, the whitewashed cottages looking down from the cliff tops, small boats in a tiny harbour, and there's that same bracing quality of the wave-wafted air. As you stroll along the rocky coastline above the low cliffs, past the two lifeboat stations and the Seawatch Centre, all thoughts are on ships and the ocean. If it's sunny and the breeze is only slight, everything appears so picturesque and peaceful, but as you read the inscriptions on the *Royal Charter* memorial, you get a different story…

A Ship in Distress

The monument remembers the night of 26 October 1859. A proud British cutter, the Royal Charter was on the last stretch of its long homeward journey from Hobson's Bay in Melbourne to Liverpool. Sailing past Ireland there had not been a hint of wind, but as night fell, a savage storm ensued. Captain Taylor signalled for a pilot, but none would come on such a night. In deep trouble, he set anchor, but at 1:30am the chain parted. At daybreak two locals saw the wreck being pounded against the rocks.

Gallant Seamen

To their horror they saw a man shimmy down a rope from the decks and into the furious sea. He had volunteered to try to swim with a hawser for shore, the only means to secure the ship and save the lives of the crew and passengers. Twice he failed, but Joseph Rogers, an able seaman from Malta, finally made it and lashed the ship to a rock. The gallant seaman and the men of Moelfre made a human chain into the breakers. They managed to rescue 18 passengers, 5 riggers and 18 crew, but on that day 452 people, including all the officers and 28 men from Moelfre, lost their lives. The ship also carried gold and, though most of it was recovered, some must still be buried among the barnacles and tangled seaweed in that watery graveyard you see below.

An Ancient Village

On the way back to Moelfre you leave the sea and follow country lanes through peaceful pastures. Through the hedges you'll spot a roofless 12th-century chapel, which you pass en route to Din Lligwy, an ancient village hidden in the woods. This is a wonderfully preserved Celtic settlement dating back to the last years of the Roman Empire in the 4th century AD.

Burial Chamber

In a field further down the lane are the remains of a neolithic burial chamber. The Lligwy tomb has a massive capstone weighing 25 tons. The excavation in 1909 revealed the remains of 15 to 30 people and Beaker and grooved ware pottery.

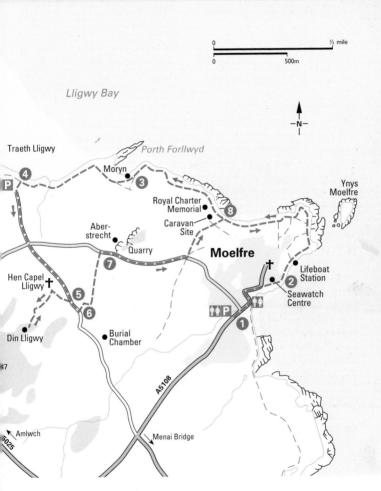

WALK 11 DIRECTIONS

❶ From the car park, follow the main road (A5108) down to the shore. The road winds behind the bay before swinging left. Leave the road at that point for a shoreline path on the right.

❷ Pass the the Seawatch Centre and the lifeboat station and ignore the footpath signs pointing inland. Instead follow a clear coast path that looks across to the island of Ynys Moelfre. After passing to the right of terraced cottages and going through a couple of kissing gates the path crosses a small caravan site. It then goes through another kissing gate and climbs past the *Royal Charter* memorial.

❸ Swinging left into Porth Forllwyd, the path ends beside a cottage, Moryn. Follow a track to a gate, turning before it along a fenced path into a field. Keep ahead to rejoin the coast, which turns in above the large bay of Traeth Lligwy.

❹ On reaching the beach car park, turn left along the narrow lane before going straight ahead at the next crossroads.

❺ Take the next path on the right, signposted to Din Lligwy ancient village. First, turn half-right across the field to see the old chapel. Then bear left across two fields and into a wood concealing Din Lligwy. Return to the lane and turn right along it.

❻ Leave after 50yds (46m) over a ladder stile on the left. Follow the doglegging boundary right to a stile, over which turn left, walking downfield to emerge by a roadside quarry at Aber-strecht.

WHAT TO LOOK OUT FOR

At Din Lligwy you enter the foundations of the old settlement through thick rubble walls, which would have been added as protection against the Romans. The circular huts inside were the living quarters, while the large rectangular hut in the top right-hand corner would have been the smelting workshop – the remains of a charcoal hearth were excavated here.

❼ Follow the lane right to the edge of the village and go left on a waymarked track. Around the first bend, swing left through a gate, keeping right at a fork to walk through the caravan site again.

❽ Follow the shoreline path back to the start.

WHERE TO EAT AND DRINK

Ann's Pantry in the village is set in a pleasant whitewashed cottage with picnic tables in a lawned garden. On the seafront you'll find the Kinmel Arms, its patio garden overlooking the pebble beach. There are bar snacks and more substantial dishes, including freshly caught fish, served at lunchtimes and in the evenings. Inside there is memorabilia associated with the village lifeboats and rescues, as well as a display featuring ensigns from different parts of the world.

Around Holyhead Mountain

The last stop before Ireland, rugged and rocky Holy Island offers some of the best walking in Anglesey.

DISTANCE *5 miles (8km)*   MINIMUM TIME *3hrs*

ASCENT/GRADIENT *1,230ft (375m)* ▲▲▲   LEVEL OF DIFFICULTY ✦✦✦

PATHS *Well-maintained paths and tracks*

LANDSCAPE *Heathland, coastal cliffs and rocky hills, 2 stiles*

SUGGESTED MAP *OS Explorer 262 Anglesey West*

START / FINISH *Grid reference: SH 210818*

DOG FRIENDLINESS *Dogs should be on lead at all times*

PARKING *RSPB car park*

PUBLIC TOILETS *Just up road from car park*

Anglesey's flat and when you motor along the fast and busy A55 to Holyhead the flat fields flashing by the car window confirm the fact. It comes as a surprise then, that when you leave the main road and pass Trearddur Bay, the green fields turn to rugged heathland that rises to a rocky hillside. The locals and the mapmakers call it Holyhead Mountain, and it matters little that it rises to a mere 722ft (220m) above the waves, because this mountain rises steep and craggy and looks out across those waves to Ireland.

Breeding Grounds

The path from the car park heads straight for a white castellated building known as Ellin's Tower. This former summerhouse is now an RSPB seabird centre. The surrounding area is a breeding ground for puffins, guillemots, razorbills and the rare mountain chough (See What to Look For): a closed-circuit video camera shows live pictures of these birds. Outside you can look across to the little island of South Stack, with its lighthouse perched on high cliffs. Although the cliff scenery is stunning, a stark, stone shelter and the microwave dishes of a BT station spoil the early scenes, but they're soon left behind as you head to that rocky 'mountain'.

Across the Heath

In this area the footpath traverses splendid maritime heath dominated by ling, bell heather and stunted western gorse. The rare spotted rock rose also grows here, it looks a little like the common rock rose but has red spots on its yellow petals. The footpath eventually climbs over the shoulder of a ridge connecting the summit and North Stack. You'll see a direct path heading for the summit when you reach this ridge. It's a bit of a scramble in places, but worth doing if you're fit and there are no young children in your party. Otherwise, the best route for the more sedate rambler is to head along the ridge towards North Stack.

North Stack

After a short climb there's a big drop down a zig-zag path to reach a rocky knoll with a splendid view down to North Stack, another tiny island. On the mainland, adjacent, there's a Fog Signal Station warning of the more treacherous waters.

The Boats to Ireland

Now the walk cuts across more heath along the north-east side of Holyhead Mountain. From here you'll be looking over Holyhead town and its huge harbour. Once a small fishing village, Holyhead came to prominence after the Act of Union 1821, when its convenient position for travel to Ireland made it the ideal choice for shipping routes. The big ferries and 'cats' will be a feature of this last leg, for you'll surely see at least one glide out of the bay.

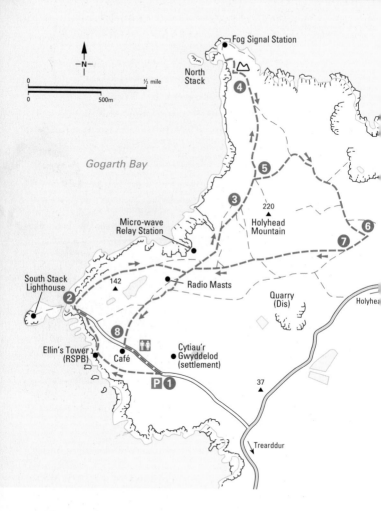

WALK 12 DIRECTIONS

❶ Take the path for the RSPB centre at Ellin's Tower, a small white castellated building, then climb along the path back to the road which should be followed along to its end.

❷ If you're not visiting the South Stack Lighthouse, climb right on a path passing a stone shelter. The path detours right to round the BT aerials and dishes. At a crossroads go left, heading back to the coast, then take the left fork. Ignore the next left, a dead

HOLYHEAD MOUNTAIN

end path and continue following waymarks over the north shoulder of Holyhead Mountain.

3 Ignore paths leading off right to the summit, but keep left on a good path heading north towards North Stack.

4 After passing through a grassy walled enclosure the path descends in zig-zags down some steep slopes. Joining a track follow it left to a rocky platform, where the Fog Signal Station and the island of North Stack come into full view. Retrace your steps back up the zig-zags and towards Holyhead Mountain.

5 At a junction below the summit path, turn sharp left across the heath. Go right at its end, contouring the eastern side of the mountain. Keep right at a fork and then ignore another summit path from the right. Beyond the mountain, take a right fork as the path comes to a wall. Follow the path downhill towards rough pastureland.

6 Go down a grassy walled track before turning right along another, similar one. This soon becomes a rough path traversing more heathland, now to the south of Holyhead Mountain.

7 Where a waymarked path is later signed off left, bear right below craggy cliffs towards the relay station. Go left at the far end but just before meeting your outward route, swing left again on another path past radio masts. Approaching a service track, bear left again on to a tarmac path. Continue with it over a stile beside a gate, emerging at the end on to the road opposite the café.

8 Turn left along the road to return to the car park.

Moel Famau: the Mother Mountain

Walk to the highest of the Clwydian Hills and see a beautiful wooded limestone valley on the way.

DISTANCE *8 miles (12.9km)*   MINIMUM TIME *4hrs 30min*

ASCENT/GRADIENT *1,608ft (490m)* ▲▲▲ LEVEL OF DIFFICULTY +++

PATHS *Well-defined paths and forestry tracks, 8 stiles*

LANDSCAPE *Heather moor, forest and farmland*

SUGGESTED MAP *OS Explorer 265 Clwydian Range*

START / FINISH *Grid reference: SJ 198625*

DOG FRIENDLINESS *Dogs could run free in forest and on heather ridges*

PARKING *Pay car park by Loggerheads Country Park Visitor Centre*

PUBLIC TOILETS *At Visitor Centre*

NOTE *Route can be shortened by taking regular Moel Famau shuttle bus, which runs on Sundays (July to September) and bank holidays, from forestry car park to Loggerheads*

If you're driving into Wales from the north-west, the chances are that the first hills you'll see are the Clwydians, dark rolling ridges that rise up from the sea at Prestatyn and decline 20 miles (32km) or so south in the fields of the Alun Valley. Although the hills are empty these days, at one time they were highly populated. Climb to the tops and you'll see Iron and Bronze Age forts scattered about the hilltops, some of them among the best preserved in Wales.

At Loggerheads

One of the best places to start a walk in the Clwydians is Loggerheads. The path from the information centre follows the shallow, swift-flowing River Alun through a narrow limestone valley filled with wych elm and oak. In July, you'll see limestone flora, including field scabious, wild thyme, rock rose and bloody cranesbill, while above there are spotted woodpeckers, tawny owls and nuthatches.

On the Top

The climb out of the valley includes a short traverse of farmland before clambering through heather fields to Moel Famau, which means 'mother mountain' and at 1,818ft (554m) is the highest of the range. The monument on the summit was built in 1810 to celebrate the jubilee of King George III. Its square tower and spire were wrecked by a violent gale some 50 years later, and the place lay in ruins until 1970 when it was tidied up. Below and to the west there's the much older site of Moel y Gaer, one of those fascinating hill-forts with concentric earthwork rings sculpted into a grassy knoll. Casting your eyes beyond the rings and across the green fields and chequered hedgerows of the Vale of Clwyd, it's interesting to pick out the familiar skyline summits of Snowdonia. Tryfan's jagged crest is easy to spot, but somehow you cannot quite see Snowdon and that's because Moel Siabod, prima donna that it feels it is, has elbowed its way to the front, to hide the real star of the show, Snowdon, and confuse the issue. Fortunately there are topographs to help you out.

MOEL FAMAU

The ridge walking from the summit is delightful, and on a good day you might wish to extend your day by doing the Walk 14 extension. Otherwise, a wide path takes you down to the forest, where it continues down a grassy ride. While the spruce trees are not an attractive habitat for a wide range of species you might easily spot a song thrush, colourful chaffinches or coal tits; or maybe, just maybe, a sparrowhawk. Country lanes and farm pastures take you down to the banks of the River Alun which guides you back to Loggerheads.

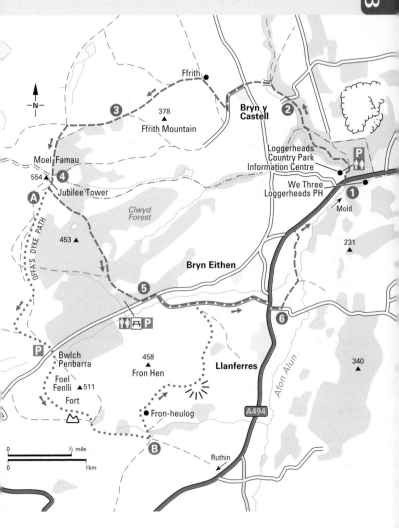

WALK 13 DIRECTIONS

❶ Go past the front of the Loggerheads Country Park Information Centre, café and other buildings, cross the bridge over the Alun and turn left along the surfaced path through the valley. Keep to the main, near-level path, marked the Leete Path.

❷ Pass the A.L.Y.N. Kennels, cross a lane, then look out for a small, often slippery path on the left (signed Moel Famau). This leads to a footbridge. Across this the path heads west, then staggers to the right across a farm lane and climbs past a farmhouse. Enclosed by thickets, it climbs to the right of another house to reach a T-junction of country lanes. Go straight ahead and follow the lane uphill, then turn right to follow the track that passes Ffrith farm before swinging left to climb round the pastured slopes of Ffrith Mountain. Take the left fork in the tracks (at grid ref 177637).

3 The route skirts a spruce plantation and climbs to a crossroads of tracks, marked by a tall waymarker post. Turn left here on a wide path over undulating heather slopes towards the tower on the top of Moel Famau.

4 From the summit, head south-east and go through a gate at the end of the wall to follow a wide track, marked with red-tipped waymarker posts, south-east along the forest's edge. The track continues its descent through the trees to meet the roadside car park/picnic area 0.75 mile

(1.2km) east of Bwlch Penbarra's summit (See Information Panel on using shuttle bus).

5 Turn left along the road, before turning right when you get to the first junction. The quiet lane leads to the busy A494. Cross the main road with care and continue along the hedge-lined lane staggered to the right.

6 A waymarked path on the left heads north-east across fields towards the banks of the Alun. Don't cross the river at the bridge, but head north, through the gateway and across more fields, passing a stone-built house below on the right. Turn right on the A494. It's just 0.5 mile (800m) from here to the Loggerheads Country Park entrance, and there are verges and paths to walk on.

The Clwydian Skyline

*A walk along the heather-clad ridges of the
Clwydian Range.*
See map and information panel for Walk 13

DISTANCE 10 miles (16.1km)	MINIMUM TIME 5hrs 30min
ASCENT/GRADIENT 1,805ft (550m) ▲▲▲	LEVEL OF DIFFICULTY +++

WALK 14 DIRECTIONS
(Walk 13 Option)

Like Walk 13, this route takes you
to the top of Moel Famau, but this
time you stay high and walk south
along the ridges that have been
designated an Area of Outstanding
Natural Beauty (AONB).

From Point ❹, ignore the
numerous tracks that descend
from the summit to the forest,
but instead stay with the wide
path, that heads south along an
undulating ridge, Point ❹, with
spruce woods to the left and gorse
bushes and the odd hawthorn tree
scattered among the heather and
patches of bracken and bilberry.
Look for the coloured Emperor
moth. The male can often be seen
fluttering fast and low over the
heather, the female only comes
out at dusk.

The wide track eventually
descends to a high roadside car
park at Bwlch Penbarra, where
you'll often see a refreshment
van. The route can be shortened
by taking the regular Moel
Famau shuttle bus, which runs on
Sundays and bank holidays, July
to September, from here back to
Loggerheads. Across the road and
the car park you can go on a direct
path to the top of Foel Fenlli, the
next hill, where you can see the
earthwork remains of an Iron Age

fort. The best route, however,
follows the Offa's Dyke Path
around the west and south sides
of the hill, passing through more
heather and lush bilberry to reach
the hill's high shoulder, alongside
the outer rings of the ancient fort.

The path descends steeply to a
small plantation, before climbing
beside its western edge. An
Offa's Dyke waymark highlights
your path which turns left along
a fence, then traces the edge of
another plantation.

You come to a gate and a
crossroads of paths, Point ❹,
south of Fron-heulog farm,
which can be seen on the
pastured hillside to the left.
Turn left through the gate and
follow the track to the top gate
just to the left of the farm.
Beyond this, swing right on a
track that skirts above the farm
and soon offers superb views of
the Alun Valley and the tiered
limestone hills beyond.

The path follows the intake wall
on the right, and arcs round the
hillside of Fron Hen, coming out
on a narrow country lane, where
you turn right and rejoin Walk 13
to return to the car park.

Archaeology at Llyn Brenig

Walking in the footsteps of prehistoric farmers and hunters.

DISTANCE *3 miles (4.8km)*	MINIMUM TIME *1hr 30min*
ASCENT/GRADIENT *394ft (120m)* ▲▲▲	LEVEL OF DIFFICULTY ✦✦✦

PATHS *Well-defined paths and farm tracks, 4 stiles*

LANDSCAPE *Sheep pastures*

SUGGESTED MAP *OS Explorer 264 Vale of Clwyd*

START / FINISH *Grid reference: SH 983574*

DOG FRIENDLINESS *Sheep country, keep dogs on leads*

PARKING *Car park on north-east side*

PUBLIC TOILETS *At car park*

WALK 15 DIRECTIONS

In days gone by Brenig was a wilderness. Here the Afon Brenig and Afon Fechan began life on the rolling heather moors of Mynydd Hiraethog, and here hardy inhabitants had tried to eke out a living on the thin peaty soils. In the 1900s Brenig came to the attention of those seeking water for Birkenhead's new industries, but the scheme didn't get the go-ahead for 70 more years.

One of the problems with flooding these valleys was that they were sites of immense archaeological interest; sites known to have been occupied since prehistoric times. Some would have to be submerged beneath the huge new lake. Before they were, however, teams from the University College of North Wales and the University of Manchester investigated 50 sites in the region. Finally completed in 1976, the reservoir is used to maintain the levels of the River Dee, which in turn is used for water abstraction.

Llyn Brenig is a huge reservoir, bordered along its eastern shore by farm pastures, inhabited since prehistoric times; and on the west by modern spruce forests and vast tracts of wild heather moorland. It's a pleasant scene, echoing to the sound of birdsong and the sight of dinghies gliding across the water. Many of the archaeological sites are linked by waymarked trails. Here we will follow a 3-mile (4.8km) route on the north-east shoreline.

Go through the gate beside the toilet block and follow the stony track to the Ring Cairn on the right. Near by is a large stone, which marks the site of a mesolithic camp, where

WHERE TO EAT AND DRINK

The Visitor Centre overlooking the dam near the south-west of the lake has a welcoming café serving simple meals, burgers, snacks, coffee and cakes. The Sportsman Inn on the A543 serves bar meals, but is only open in the evening.

archaeologists found flint tools and charcoal from *c*5700 BC. The settlers were the first after the ice age and would have been hunter-gatherers from the coast. Their visits were seasonal at first. The Ring Cairn itself was used for ceremonial purposes and would have consisted of a stone ring, surrounded by carved posts.

WHILE YOU'RE THERE

Drive round to the Visitor Centre on the west side of the reservoir, near to the dam. There's a permanent exhibition and you can view a video on the life of Brenig.

Near by, you can see a burial mound, built by the later Bronze Age settlers. Known as Boncyn Arian (the Money Hillock) this barrow dates back to 1600 BC. Digging revealed six cremation burials; one of the urns held the burnt ear bones of a child.

Go back a few paces to a stile by a gate on the opposite side of the track and strike up the hill past a marker towards the forest skyline. You reach the remains of Hafotai settlement; formerly huts, thatched with heather and rushes, they were summer dwellings for 16th-century farmers.

The way now turns south beside the forest, following occasional markers to a gate by a stream. Head up to another marker and then swing right across a field system, which probably belongs to the Bronze Age, to reach the Platform Cairn. This topped the burial site of an adult and child and was originally a wide ring with an open centre, the inner edge highlighted by upright stones. A central post hole was later covered by a stone platform.

WHAT TO LOOK OUT FOR

Above the Kerb Cairn is Maen Cleddau, the Swords' Stone, a huge erratic boulder with a broken fragment. Deposited here in the last ice age, its name comes from a legend in which the fragment was sliced off by a sword-wielding giant.

From the Platform Cairn, descend the slopes to Hen Ddinbych, which means Old Denbigh. The ditches hereabouts are the remains of a medieval field system. You can see the remnants of what was probably once a large farm or even a small village – some say it was the site of old Denbigh but that is doubtful. It has been suggested that here is the site of a Roman camp or a pre-Norman church and churchyard. Although digging took place in 1956, the site was only partially excavated and the mystery remains. Turn left to follow a fence, parallel to and beneath the south side of the forest, then go over a stile on to the bracken moor. Bear left on a trod that leads across a stream to a Bronze Age burial site in the valley bottom. The Kerb Cairn was built over the remains of a prehistoric hut, its post holes marked by wooden posts.

Retrace your steps to the stile and alongside the fence, but beyond Hen Ddinbych, bear right, climbing past markers to reach another Bronze Age cairn. The path now swings right to join a bulldozed track leading past Hafoty Siôn Llwyd, a now abandoned and rapidly crumbling farmhouse that was rebuilt in 1881 using stone taken from the buildings at Hen Ddinbych. On reaching the main round-the-lake track, turn right and follow it back to the car park.

The Bard Taliesin and the Twin Lakes

Here you can discover two very different lakes, one to inspire poets present and one that inspired bards of the past.

DISTANCE *5 miles (8km)* MINIMUM TIME *3hrs*

ASCENT/GRADIENT *984ft (300m)* ▲▲▲ LEVEL OF DIFFICULTY ✦✦✦

PATHS *Clear paths and forestry tracks, 5 stiles*

LANDSCAPE *Lake, afforested hillsides and woods*

SUGGESTED MAP *OS Explorer OL17 Snowdon*

START / FINISH *Grid reference: SH 756618*

DOG FRIENDLINESS *Dogs could run free in forest areas*

PARKING *Forestry pay car park, north of Llyn Crafnant*

PUBLIC TOILETS *At car park*

Llyn Crafnant is serenely beautiful, and it's only 5 minutes from the car to its northern tip. Here, at the head of the 'valley of garlic', is a lake surrounded by woodland, lush pasture and craggy hills. The walk is easy too, on an undulating forestry track that gives a slightly elevated view of the lake. Little whitewashed cottages are arranged neatly in the lower pastures, while the hill slopes at the head of the valley are tinged with the russet of heather and the golden grey of the much-faulted crags which rise to the knobbly ridge crest. Here the summit of Crimpiau rules supreme.

The Dead Lake

After rounding the lake the route climbs out of the valley, through the trees and zig-zags down into the upland hollow of Llyn Geirionydd. This is a wilder place altogether, one with barren hillsides and conifer plantations – sometimes there are waterskiers on the lake to contradict the wildness. Another lakeside path follows, sometimes almost dipping into the lapping waters. Scaling a bluff you come to the spoil heaps of a huge old lead mine, one of many in the area. The lake has a secret – it has been poisoned by these lead mines – you'll see no fish here!

Taliesin and the Kings

On a grassy mound at the end of the lake stands an obelisk. Erected in 1850 it commemorates Taliesin, a 6th-century bard who has been linked to legends as colourful as his poems. Most scholars believe him to be of Irish descent and it is known he lived here at the northern end of Geirionydd. In those times bards would have been resident in the courts of many warlord kings, and Taliesin was said to have attended King Maelgwyn Gwynedd, one of the most sinful rulers in history, according to one of the local monks. After a fiery row the departing bard predicted that a yellow creature would rise from Morfa Rhianedd (Llandudno) and kill the King. It is known that when the King died in AD 547 there was an outbreak of yellow fever. Many of Taliesin's more fanciful poems recall tales of magic and mystery, and many of them relate to the heroics of the great King Arthur, who some believe was his one-time master. It is quite possible that he spent time in the court of Urien of Rheged, a northern leader whose kingdom occupied much of modern Cumbria and south-west Scotland. Many people link Urien's deeds with those of the mythical Arthur.

The bardic traditions didn't die with Taliesin, for the Welsh poet, Gwilim Cowlyd organised an Eisteddfod in 1863, after a disagreement with the rules of the national event. It was held here until 1912, eight years after Cowlyd's death, and each year attracted many distinguished entries.

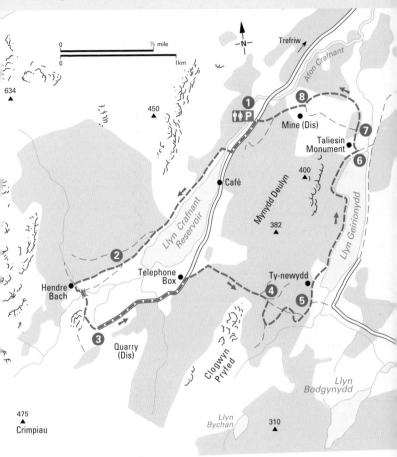

WALK 16 DIRECTIONS

1 Turn right out of the car park and follow the lane to the north end of Llyn Crafnant. Turn right again here, and follow the forestry track along the north-west shores of the lake, before taking the lower left fork.

2 Ignore a stile on the left, and instead climb with the forestry track. Keep watching for a later waymarked footpath on which you should descend left to cross a stream by a cottage, Hendre Bach. Turn left down a track passing a couple of modern chalets.

49

③ Turn left along the road which heads back towards the lake. Leave this at a telephone box for a path, signposted 'Llyn Geirionydd' and waymarked with blue-capped posts. This climbs through the conifer forests and over the shoulder of Mynydd Deulyn.

WHERE TO EAT AND DRINK

There's a good café at Llyn Crafnant, though it's on the wrong side of the lake for en route refreshments. The Fairy Falls Hotel in Trefriw is a pleasant old world inn with a friendly atmosphere. You can have a traditional bar meal or eat in the Cottage Bar Restaurant. They also serve morning coffee and afternoon tea.

④ Descend with the main winding forestry track, still following the obvious blue-capped posts. Ignore the track forking to the right – it leads to Llyn Bychan.

⑤ On reaching the valley floor, leave the track to go over a step stile on the left. The path crosses a couple of meadows beneath Ty-newydd cottage before tracing Llyn Geirionydd's shoreline. At

WHILE YOU'RE THERE

The Trefriw Woollen Mill uses the head of water from Crafnant and Geirionydd to generate its electricity and has been producing woollen goods for 150 years. These days the shop and turbine house are open to the public Monday to Saturday throughout the year and on summer Sundays.

the northern end of the lake the path keeps to the right of a wall and meets a farm track.

⑥ Turn left and immediately right to reach the Taliesin Monument on a grassy mound. Descend to a green path heading north towards the Crafnant Valley.

⑦ Veer left to cross a ladder stile and follow the undulating path ahead over wooded rock and heather knolls.

⑧ The path eventually swings left to reach an old mine. Here, take the lower track on the right which descends back to the valley road and the forest car park.

WHAT TO LOOK OUT FOR

Though the lead mines have poisoned the lake, two quite rare plants thrive on rocks from the spoil heaps. The forked spleenwort looks like a cross between grass and a moss, but is actually a fern. It doesn't seem to mind the high toxicity, and neither does the alpine pennycress, a short hairless perennial with untoothed leaves growing stalkless from the stem and with clusters of small white/pale mauve flowers that appear between April and July.

Dolgarrog's Tragic Disaster Area

Discovering grim secrets from the 19th century, high in one of the Carneddau's loneliest valleys.

WALK 17

DISTANCE 7 miles (11.3km) **MINIMUM TIME** 3hrs 30min

ASCENT/GRADIENT 500ft (152m) ▲▲▲ **LEVEL OF DIFFICULTY** +++

PATHS Tracks and country lanes, 5 stiles

LANDSCAPE Uncultivated moor, rough pasture and crag

SUGGESTED MAP OS Explorer OL17 Snowdon

START / FINISH Grid reference: SH 731663

DOG FRIENDLINESS Dogs should be on leads

PARKING Car park at the end of road

PUBLIC TOILETS None en route

It was an ordinary Saturday evening in Dolgarrog, it had been raining hard for a few days, but in November that's not so unusual.

Disaster in the Hills

In the hills something was wrong. In the dark of night there were tremors in the ground and groans coming from the deep hollow of Eigiau. The reservoir dam was moving. Suddenly cracks appeared… then the unthinkable happened. The waters came thundering out through broken stone into the wide upper valley of the Afon Porth-llwyd, picking up speed towards the Coedty Reservoir. Would that hold? No, the dam disintegrated under the ever-increasing power of the flood. Boulders weighing over 200 tons were gouged from the mountainsides and thrust down in the raging torrents, and down further, towards the hapless village of Dolgarrog. Cottages lying in the way were smashed and the furnace at the aluminium works was engulfed, resulting in violent explosions. Dolgarrog was devastated.

Death Toll

Sixteen lives were lost that night in 1925. It is said that the death toll would have been higher were it not for the fact that many of the villagers and their children were at the cinema, which was on higher ground. An inquiry found that the dam had been built on insecure moraine debris from the last ice age, and had shifted under the pressure of the reservoir's headwater. The dam was never rebuilt and the lake is now quite shallow, some 14ft (4.3m) lower than its previous level.

From Dolgarrog you drive up a winding little road, through that narrow gorge, past the rebuilt cottages to arrive at the car park beneath the dam. Eigiau today is austere and rugged. You're in a sombre rushy basin deep in the Carneddau's heartlands. The crags that rise out of this sad and shallow lake are precipitous. There's a whitewashed cottage beneath a crag by the dam and another disused one up the valley. The view ends in the darkness of a steep grassy gully plummeting from the pass, Bwlch y Tri Marchog. The summit of Carnedd Llewelyn is hidden from here, though you'll see it later from the other side of the valley, but Foel Grach, Foel-fras and Drum all look down on the scene from the western skies.

All is Peaceful

From the dam a pleasing green road takes you back, the way the water would have gone, to Coedty Reservoir where you can look down to the Conwy Valley. You can still see the mess of boulders by the oak-shaded river banks, some of them undisturbed since that fateful evening. All is peaceful. In fact it's just an ordinary day in Dolgarrog.

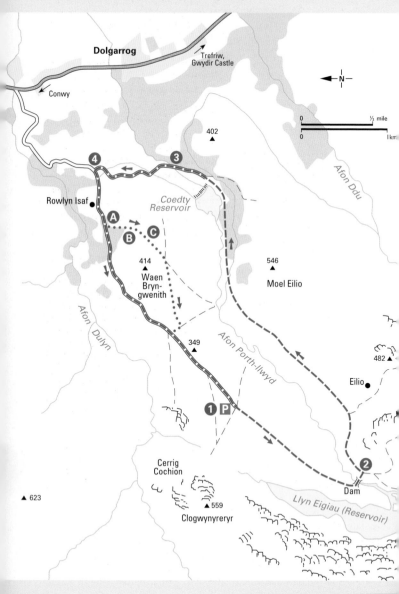

WALK 17 DIRECTIONS

1 Follow the track heading roughly south-west from the car park into the jaws of Eigiau. This turns left below the main dam and goes over a bridge across the reservoir's outflow stream.

2 Turn left along the greener track that runs above and parallel to the river, ignoring the path on the right beneath Eilio. The gated track passes Coedty Reservoir and then leads to a country lane by the dam.

3 Follow the lane as it descends to cross the river, then climbs out on to the hillside high above the Conwy Valley.

4 Turn left at the T-junction to Rowlyn Isaf farm. The quickest and the recommended route follows the quiet country lane back to the car park.

AN ALTERNATIVE ROUTE

It is possible to get back by using the path south of Waen Bryn-gwenith. However it's very rough in the early stages where the path is lost in thick bracken. For the purist however a signposted path from the woods, Point **A**, beyond the farm climbs beside a wall and fades near the top end of the woods.

Here look out for a small gate on the left, Point **B**. Now you have to fight through thick bracken (easier in winter) to reach the next field where you find a gate beside a ruin, Point **C**. Go left, then follow the contours round right, and keep above a longitudinal fence/wall. Nearing the road, cross a ladder stile then turn right to another one by the road. Turn left along the road to the start.

Overleaf: Llyn Idwal (Walk 18)

WALK 18

A Taming Walk in the Devil's Kitchen

Explore the most perfect hanging valley in Snowdonia, its rock ledges and hanging gardens.

DISTANCE *3 miles (4.8km)*   MINIMUM TIME *2hrs 30min*

ASCENT/GRADIENT *1,378ft (420m)* ▲▲▲ LEVEL OF DIFFICULTY ✛✛✛

PATHS *Well-defined paths*

LANDSCAPE *High mountain cwm*

SUGGESTED MAP *OS Explorer OL17 Snowdon*

START / FINISH *Grid reference: SH 649603*

DOG FRIENDLINESS *Dogs should be on lead*

PARKING *Small pay car park at Ogwen; others along Llyn Ogwen*

PUBLIC TOILETS *At car park*

Shepherds say that Idwal is the haunt of demons and no bird dares fly over its damned water. In the 18th century, writer Thomas Pennant came here and said it was 'a place to inspire murderous thoughts, environed with horrible precipices', and it was here in the 12th century that Idwal, son of Owain Gwynedd, was brutally murdered by Dunawd, in whose care he had been entrusted.

Menacing Atmosphere

If you come to this place on a day when the damp mountain mists swirl in and out of the blackened mossy crags, and when rain-soaked waterfalls drop from those mists like plumes of steam, you will experience the atmospheric menace. However, the sunshine can paint a very different picture, with golden rocks that are a playground for the modern-day climber and small mountain birds such as the wheatear and ring ouzel flitting through the breeze-blown grasses.

A Perfect Hanging Valley

Cwm Idwal is a perfect hanging valley, and a fine place to study geology and nature. In the last ice age a small glacier would have been slowly scouring its way over the cliffs at the head of the cwm before joining the huge glacier that used to fill the U-shaped valley of Nant Ffrancon. You will pass the moraines (the debris left behind by the glacier) not long after leaving the car park at Ogwen.

The glaciation left a legacy in Idwal, for here in the inaccessible places free from animal grazing, rare plant species are to be found. These brought botanists from far and wide. Their favoured spots were the crags around Twll Du, otherwise known as the Devil's Kitchen, a deep defile where the mountainside's volcanic bedrock is divided by a column of basalt. Here was the snout of the glacier and, on the surrounding ledges and crevices, the rich soils allowed many species of Arctic plants to flourish. The most famous is the rare Snowdon lily, discovered in the 17th century by Edward Llwyd. Tufted and Arctic saxifrage are also here, but hard to spot, but the starry and mossy saxifrages are there for all to see, as are wood sorrel, wood anemone and oak ferns. Collectively, the foliage seems to flow down the rocks and you can see why it's called the Hanging Gardens.

Lofty Viewpoint

Climbing above the rocks the path attains a wild and windswept hollow of moor grass and rushes. Llyn y Cwn (dog lake) is a shallow pool tucked beneath the loose boulder and shale slopes of Glyder Fawr. In summer bogbean rings the pool's outer edges with its pale pink blooms. This is a fine lofty place to dwell and admire the mountain views before going back down to the cauldron of Idwal.

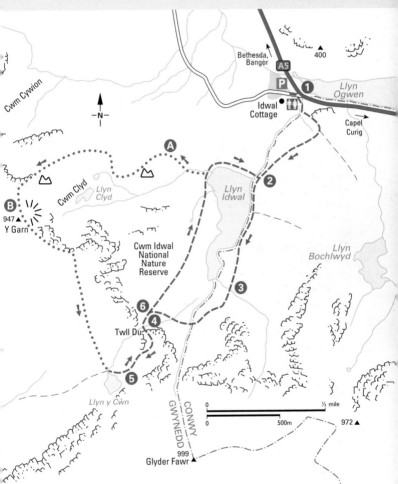

WALK 18 DIRECTIONS

❶ The Cwm Idwal nature trail starts to the left of the toilet block at Ogwen and climbs up the hillside to pass some impressive waterfalls before turning right and continuing up the hill.

❷ Go through a gate in a fence, that marks the boundary of the National Nature Reserve, and turn

57

left along the side of Llyn Idwal's eastern shores. The clear footpath climbs into the dark shadows of Cwm Idwal.

3 Now you leave the nature trail, which turns right to complete a circuit around the lake. Instead ascend beneath the rock climbing grounds of the Idwal Slabs and across the stream of Nant Ifan, beyond which the footpath zig-zags up rough boulder ground to the foot of Twll Du – the Devil's Kitchen. If the weather, and the forecast too, are fine climb to Llyn y Cwn at the top of this impressive defile, if not, skip this bit and go to Point **6**.

4 To ascend Twll Du climb the engineered path as it angles left up the rock face, which will now be on your right-hand side, above an extensive area of scree and boulder. At the top you come to a relatively gentle (by comparison) grassy hollow between the rising

summits of Y Garn, to the right, and Glyder Fawr, to the left.

5 Just beyond the first grassy mounds you come across the small tarn of Llyn y Cwn – the dog lake – which makes a great picnic spot. Now retrace your steps carefully to the bottom of Twll Du.

6 Among some huge boulders, the path forks and the left branch heads down to run above the western shore of Llyn Idwal, then rounds its northern end to meet the outward route at Point **2**. Now follow the route of your outward journey back to the car park at Ogwen.

Climbing the Eminence

*If the forecast and conditions are fine, take the opportunity to climb
to Y Garn, one of the finest peaks in the Glyder Range.*
See map and information panel for Walk 18

WALK 19

| DISTANCE 5 miles (8km)   MINIMUM TIME 4hrs |
| ASCENT/GRADIENT 2,230ft (680m) ▲▲▲   LEVEL OF DIFFICULTY +++ |

WALK 19 DIRECTIONS

(Walk 18 Option)

When you stand on the shores of Llyn Ogwen and look up to the Glyder skyline, one mountain stands out; not the highest in the range, but one that has the powerful profile of an Everest, an Eiger, or Jungfrau. It's known as Y Garn, which in Welsh means the eminence, and its summit is well worth the effort of the climb.

Follow Walk 18 to Llyn Idwal, Point ❷, but this time turn right over the bridge across the outflow stream and trace the northern shore of the lake. Leave the main path to strike off along a narrow westbound path heading for the base of Y Garn's north-east ridge.

From a gate a well-defined path climbs Y Garn's north-east spur, Point ❹. The path veers left into the lower regions of Cwm Clyd before curving right, back to the crest of the ridge. The middle section is very steep and the zig-zag path is eroded by walkers' shortcuts. In the upper regions the ridge narrows with precipitous drops into Cwm Clyd and Cwm Cywion.

The final steep section is climbed on the left side. At its top turn left to climb to the summit, Point ❸.

If Y Garn looks impressive from Ogwen, then the view back is even more impressive. Three lakes dominate the view, and all are on different landings of this mountain staircase. On the top there's the mountain tarn, Llyn Clyd, which looks so solemn in its shady rock-strewn cwm; then there's Idwal in its wide eerie hollow. Below that, in wide rough pastures, lies the sprawling Llyn Ogwen, at the start of the walk, with motorists speeding by oblivious on the busy A5. You cannot fail to be impressed by Ogwen's prized landmark, Tryfan, whose mighty buttresses and scree slopes completely overshadow the comparatively dull Carneddau whalebacks.

From the summit, descend on either of two paths to Llyn y Cwn, Point ❺, a small tarn that occupies a high grassy pass between Ogwen and Nant Peris. There's a path up the loose slopes of Glyder Fawr beyond, but our route takes a broad path going left to the Idwal edge, high above the rocky cwm. It descends Twll Du with the route of Walk 18, follows the western side of the lake, then descends to Ogwen via Point ❷.

Caernarfon: the Grand Tour

Walk around the castle, the narrow streets and Roman Segontium.

DISTANCE 3.5 miles (5.7km)   MINIMUM TIME 2hrs

ASCENT/GRADIENT Negligible ▲▲▲   LEVEL OF DIFFICULTY +++

PATHS Lanes and streets   NOTE Wear your shoes

LANDSCAPE Town with sea views

SUGGESTED MAP OS Explorer 263 Anglesey East

START / FINISH Grid reference: SH 480633

DOG FRIENDLINESS No restrictions except traffic

PARKING Large car park between Victoria Docks and Morrison's, north-east side of town

PUBLIC TOILETS In town centre

WALK 20 DIRECTIONS

From the south-west corner of the car park, walk through or round a new development to Victoria Dock, now a marina. The waters beyond are the Menai Strait and on the far side lie the flat green fields of the Isle of Anglesey.

Beyond the docks follow the promenade, outside the town walls, past the twin-towered Port-yr-Aur, the Golden Gate, which sports a plaque to Lionel Brabazon-Rees VC.

Continuing along the promenade you come to the north end of Caernarfon Castle, of which we'll see more later, and an old swing bridge across the Afon Seiont, the Saint River. Cross the bridge and turn left down the lane for a view of the castle.

Shortcut: backtrack from here, recross the bridge and continue around the castle to meet the town walls again. Continue down Hole in the Wall Street to rejoin

the main walk. This abbreviated route of little more than 1 mile (1.6km) takes in all the highlights except for the visit to Segontium.

The lane winds past a campsite and out into the country for almost 1 mile (1.6km) before meeting the A487 at a junction shared with another minor road.

Cross the main road, then cross the old bridge over the Seiont, now reserved for foot traffic. Follow the old road round left then, opposite a hospital entrance, drop down left by a cycleway sign (Lon Gwyrfa). Pass under the flyover, cross the Welsh Highland Railway and follow the cycle track alongside. Continue on the pavement to the railway terminus and cross a footbridge here. Take

WHERE TO EAT AND DRINK

The Black Boy Inn, Northgate Street, is a 15th-century pub with oak-beamed ceilings. They do a wide range of traditional bar meals and favourites such as a Thai green curry.

the street straight ahead: it has no sign, but quickly leads into Stryd Garnon. At its top meet the A487 again, and cross using an underpass. Go left up steps and up Tithebarn Street (Stryd y Degwm) past the Eagles pub towards the Roman fort of Segontium.

WHILE YOU'RE THERE

Between May and October you could take a cruise along the Menai Strait on the *Queen of the Sea* or the *Snowdon Queen*. The booking office is on the Quayside, Slate Quay, near the castle.

The fort lies at the far end and entrance is free. The fine museum shows Roman-era artefacts and interprets the site. Segontium was built in AD 77, shortly after the governor of Britain, Ganeus Julius Agricola, had conquered the Ordovices of Wales.

At its height the fort of Segontium would have housed 1,000 troops, all non-Roman citizens. Excavated coins show that the Romans Segontium until about AD 394.

Retrace your steps down Tithebarn Street and through the subway. This time go past the Ex-Service Club and follow Pool Street, lined with shops, to Castle Square; at its far end are the castle and the town walls. Turn right along the far side of the town walls along Hole in the Wall Street. By the junction with High Street you'll find the East Gate and its Bell Tower. In times gone by these bells would sound the curfew. If the inhabitants were not inside by 8pm, they would be locked out until 6am.

Turn left on High Street and left again down Palace Street, famous at one time for its 14 taverns.

Here you'll pass the Market Hall, formerly Plas Mawr. Most of the roof timber came from old ships and the association with the sea is reinforced when an old ship's bell peals the start of the day's trading. Turn right along Castle Ditch; the castle entrance is opposite.

Caernarfon Castle is the most imposing of Edward I's 'iron ring', designed to subdue the native Welsh. Begun in 1283, it was to become a royal palace and as such was designed to reflect its dominance over the local populace. Its mighty polygonal towers are remarkably intact. It made a grand setting for Prince Charles' investiture as Prince of Wales in 1969, almost 700 years after Edward made his son the first English Prince of Wales in the same place. The castle also houses the regimental museum of the Royal Welch Fusiliers.

Continue down Castle Ditch past the tourist information centre to the imposing 19th-century County Hall. Turn right by the side of the hall and adjoining gaol, to follow Shirehall Street past the modern administrative buildings. Beyond St Mary's Church, go through the gateway out to Victoria Dock where you retrace your steps to the car park.

WHAT TO LOOK OUT FOR

Near the end of the walk you come to St Mary's Church, founded in 1307 as a garrison church and built by Henry of Ellerton. It was almost entirely rebuilt in 1814 but some of the internal arcades remain from the earlier building, as does the Jesse Window in the southern wall.

Idyllic Valle Crucis and Dinas Bran

*From the Dee to the Eglwyseg, this walk discovers a fascinating
tapestry of history and landscape.*

DISTANCE 6.75 miles (10.9km)	**MINIMUM TIME** 4hrs

ASCENT/GRADIENT 1,296ft (395m) ▲▲▲   **LEVEL OF DIFFICULTY** +++

PATHS Tow path, farm tracks and field paths, 5 stiles

LANDSCAPE Pastoral and wooded hillsides with limestone scenery

SUGGESTED MAP OS Explorer 255 Llangollen and Berwyn

START / FINISH Grid reference: SJ 214420

DOG FRIENDLINESS On lead on farmland and country lanes.
Can run free on canal tow path

PARKING Long-stay car park in East Street, just south-west of the bridge

PUBLIC TOILETS At car park

The River Dee is never more attractive than in the Vale of Llangollen where it meanders around small but shapely hills, through forest and field, and beneath terraces of limestone. Llangollen town has prospered with all this beauty, and today is a bustling holiday resort based on an impressive five-arched bridge over the Dee – one of the seven wonders of Wales. Watching over the town there's a mysterious ruined castle, Dinas Bran, the fort of the crows.

Strolling by the Canal
This walk explores the countryside around the town and starts with a stroll along the canal. Colourful barges, some horse drawn, still cruise down the waters where there are swans and hungry ducks to persuade you to share your sandwiches. When it's time to leave them behind you enter the little valley of the Eglwyseg.

The Abbey
A short distance along this valley, the walk comes to the ruined abbey of Valle Crucis, a name that means simply valley of the cross. The cross concerned used to be on top of the Pillar of Eliseg, now sadly a rather degraded roadside relic, but once an elegant memorial to Eliseg, a ninth-century Prince of Powys. Established in 1201 by Cistercian monks from Strata Marcella near Welshpool, Valle Crucis Abbey was beautifully sited in fertile pastures, where the monks could grow crops and tend sheep. A modern caravan site has been sited next to the ruins, but the abbey is still impressive, with many original features surviving the ravages of time and the Reformation. The chapter house still has its impressive rib-vaulted roof, the windows of the east wall still reflect perfectly in the monks' fish pond, and the west front still boasts an elaborate carved doorway and a beautiful rose window.

Climbing to the Fort of the Crows
The walk climbs out of the valley to a little country lane, which takes you alongside the foot of Creigiau Eglwyseg, as fine a parade of tiered limestone

crags as you'll see in any Yorkshire dale. But the best comes last, for facing those crags is Dinas Bran, that shapely hill with the fort on top. When you get to the top, the ruins are large and impressive. Unlike Conwy, Harlech and Caernarfon, this is a true Welsh castle, probably built for those same indigenous Princes of Powys. Built on the strategic site of an existing Iron Age fort – you can still see the old embankment – the castle never played a major role in battle. Its exact demise is unknown, but historians believe that the Welsh occupiers fled before the troops of Edward I laid it to waste.

It's a fine viewpoint too. The fields of Eglwyseg seem to have a green velvet quality, framed to perfection by those limestone crags, and there's a bird's-eye view of Llangollen, sitting snugly beneath the foothills of the Berwyn.

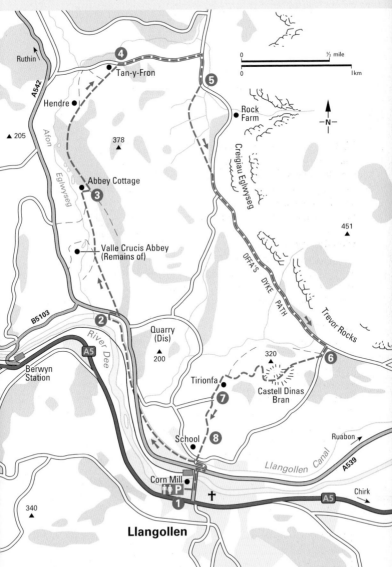

WALK 21

WALK 21 DIRECTIONS

1 Walk from the car park to the main street and go left over Llangollen Bridge. Turn right and then left, climbing to the canal and dropping on to the tow path by the café.

2 After about a mile (1.6km) the canal veers left. Leave the tow path to cross the canal on an ivy-clad bridge. Turn right along the pavement of the main road (A542). Cross the road and take a farm track signed 'FP to Valle Crucis'. The track heads north past the old abbey, where the track ends. A footpath continues, along the left edge of a field.

WHAT TO LOOK OUT FOR

Dinas Bran's name means castle of the crows and Britain's largest crow, the raven, is common here. This large black bird has a huge black beak, long tail and broad, fingered wings. It's gregarious, with a gruff croak and can often be seen haranguing buzzards in an attempt to make them drop their prey.

3 After crossing the stile at Abbey Cottage turn right for a few paces, then left to follow a well-defined track through woodland. When you get to Hendre farm take the right-hand fork leading to a narrow lane at Tan-y-Fron.

4 Turn right along the road, heading towards the prominent cliffs of Eglwyseg, then right again, along the lane that hugs the foot of the cliffs.

5 After 0.25 mile (400m), leave through the second of adjacent gates on the right. Walk away beside successive fields, crossing a stile by farm sheds on to a track back through to the lane. Go right past a junction.

6 When you reach the second junction take the right-hand fork for a few paces, then go through the gate on the right, on to a waymarked footpath leading to Castell Dinas Bran. From the crumbling west walls of the castle descend on a zig-zag path. Go around the right-hand side of a little knoll at the bottom of the hill to join a track near a house called Tirionfa.

WHILE YOU'RE THERE

Try a 2-hour trip from Llangollen Wharf on the *Thomas Telford* narrow boat, which cruises along the Llangollen Canal, through the beautiful valley of the Dee and across Telford's masterpiece, the Pontcysyllte Aqueduct.

7 At a junction, keep ahead to a second cottage, there crossing a stile into a field. Trace the left-hand edge of the field down to a narrow lane.

8 Across this, the route continues along a contained path, passing a school before crossing a road and then the Llangollen Canal close to the start of the walk. Descend the road down to Llangollen Bridge before crossing back into the car park.

WHERE TO EAT AND DRINK

There's a café at Llangollen Wharf serving sandwiches, cakes and simple meals and snacks. Alternatively, try the Corn Mill, on the south bank west of the bridge. On offer are mouthwatering steaks, fresh seafood and rich pastas, followed by desserts like bread and butter pudding with clotted cream.

Horseshoe Falls and the Velvet Hill

This is probably the prettiest walk in the whole book, and the Velvet Hill is very aptly named.

DISTANCE *3.5 miles (5.6km)*   MINIMUM TIME *2hrs*

ASCENT/GRADIENT *902ft (275m)* ▲▲▲   LEVEL OF DIFFICULTY +++

PATHS *Field paths in valley and on hillside, 10 stiles*

LANDSCAPE *Rolling hillsides, woodland and riverside pastures*

SUGGESTED MAP *OS Explorer 255 Llangollen & Berwyn*

START / FINISH *Grid reference: SJ 198433*

DOG FRIENDLINESS *Farm pastures – dogs need to be on lead*

PARKING *Picnic site and car park at Llantysilio Green on minor road north of Berwyn Station*

PUBLIC TOILETS *At car park*

At the picnic site at Llantysilio Green, just outside Llangollen, there's an idyllic spot where the Dee, enshrouded by trees, squeezes its way between the beautifully named Velvet Hill and the wooded hillside of Bryniau-mawr Bank. Yet the moment you leave the site and descend to the banks of the Dee you realise you're not quite in the countryside yet. Through those trees you can see the back of the Chain Bridge Hotel, the paraphernalia of the rejuvenated Llangollen Railway at Berwyn Station, and the Llangollen Canal.

The Horseshoe Falls

The canal ends after a short distance and you cross the meadows by the banks of the Dee. Just upstream are the Horseshoe Falls. Though they're an impressive and maybe graceful piece of engineering, many visitors feel a bit let down that the falls are just a weir and not nature's own creation. Set on a natural curve of the river, the weir was Thomas Telford's solution to harnessing the waters of the Dee to feed and control the levels of the Llangollen and Ellesmere canals.

Beyond the falls the walk climbs to Llantysilio's little church, which has its origins in the 7th century, though much of the structure was added between the 18th and 19th centuries. There's a plaque in memory of poet, Robert Browning, who worshipped here in 1886 with his friends, the Martins of Bryntysilio Hall. At the time he was staying at the Royal Hotel in Llangollen. A tractor track takes you above the tree tops, then a sheep track leads you along the hillside of Pen-y-bryn, with views of both the Dee and its tributary the Eglwyseg opening up before you.

A Recent Disaster

A section of remade path beyond a quarry incline gives you a hint of something from the recent past. November 2000 saw violent storms all over Wales. This hillside was subjected to a massive landslide following days of torrential rain. Eyewitnesses reported that an 8ft (2.4m) high torrent of mud came tumbling down the hill. It carved up the main Horseshoe Pass road, causing a blockage that would last many months, and engulfed the Britannia Inn, leaving the landlord with a £200,000 repair bill.

Hill with a View

On Velvet Hill you should see wondrous landscapes in a hundred shades of green. The Dee, now far below, meanders in crazy horseshoes. It's joined by the Afon Eglwyseg which flows beneath the gleaming terraces of limestone that shares its name. In the valley bottom beneath the crags, the Cistercian abbey of Valle Crucis seems diminutive in this big scene, as does the romantic castle-topped hill of Dinas Bran. It seems a shame to ever come down.

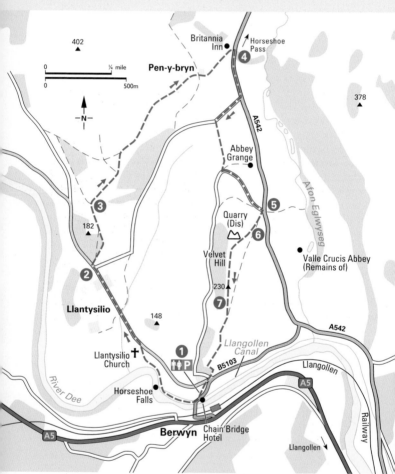

WALK 22 DIRECTIONS

① From the car park walk down to the road, turn right for a few paces then descend some steps to the back of the Chain Bridge

Hotel. Turn right to follow the path between the river and the canal. Through a kissing gate at the end of the canal you traverse riverside fields past the Horseshoe Falls and climb to Llantysilio

HORSESHOE FALLS

church. On reaching the road, turn left through the hamlet of Llantysilio to reach a junction.

2 Continue a few paces further to find a stile on the right and then climb along a rutted track, which keeps a forest to the left, then climbs north on a high pastured hillside.

3 Over a stile at the top of the field the path swings right above a plantation. Keep right at a fork and later cross a stile before eventually descending to cottages at Pen-y-bryn. An enclosed path drops to a stile, which leads out to the Horseshoe Pass road at Britannia Inn.

4 Turn right along the road, then right again when you get to the first junction. At a bend, mount a stile on the left to head south across the fields. Reaching a farm track briefly go right, leaving at a fork over a stile on the left on to a narrow lane. Go left here to meet the Horseshoe Pass road again.

5 Go over a stile on the right-hand side of the road, signposted to the Velvet Hill, and ascend by quarry workings.

6 Later, swing right along a wide grassy track climbing steeply through bracken to reach the ridge, and go left for the summit.

7 Descend south on a narrow footpath to reach a fence above some woods. Do not cross (as many have done), but follow the fence down left to a stile. After crossing the stile go right, along a path that leads back to the lane near the car park.

An Alpine Journey Above the Llugwy

Discovering the valley where rocks and the mountains are still all important.

DISTANCE 4 miles (6.4km)   MINIMUM TIME 2hrs

ASCENT/GRADIENT 295ft (90m) ▲▲▲   LEVEL OF DIFFICULTY +++
(doesn't include pinnacle scramble)

PATHS Generally clear and surfaced but can be wet in places, 9 stiles

LANDSCAPE Woodland, wetland and high pasture

SUGGESTED MAP OS Explorer OL17 Snowdon

START / FINISH Grid reference: SJ 720582

DOG FRIENDLINESS Dogs should be on lead

PARKING Behind Joe Brown's shop at Capel Curig

PUBLIC TOILETS By Joe Brown's shop

'I descended a great steep into Glan Llugwy, a bottom watered by the Llugwy, fertile in grass and varied by small groves of young oaks… The small church of Capel Curig, and a few scattered houses give life to this dreary tract. YrWyddfa and all his sons, Crib Goch, Crib y Ddysgl, Lliwedd,Yr Aran and many others here burst at once into full view and make this the finest approach to our boasted Alps'

Thomas Pennant
A Tour in Wales, 1778

The description holds true today, for nowhere that I know has one village been so strung out – Capel Curig's sparse cottages and inns stretch 6 miles (9.7km) between Pont-Cyfyng, beneath Moel Siabod, to the Pen y Gwryd, beneath Glyder Fawr. And the link still lies in those alps. The well-spaced inns were there, at first to serve the quarrymen from the barracks of Siabod and the miners from the copper mines of Snowdon, then, when the mines and quarries shut down, that new breed of visitor, the walker and the climber. These inns were a convenient meeting place. Geoffrey Winthrop Young was one of the first, but many followed, pioneering new routes on the crags. Quickly Capel Curig became the Zermatt of Wales, and Snowdon, the Matterhorn. In the 1950s the Pen y Gwryd Inn, run by enthusiast Chris Biggs, became a centre for planning Alpine and Himalayan expeditions. Here Lord Hunt and his team, who in 1953 were the first to climb Everest, met to make the final preparations before departing for Nepal. The Climbers' Bar has a wood ceiling that has been autographed by many world famous climbers, including the summit pair, Sir Edmund Hillary and Tenzing Norgay.

While Walk 24 will take you to one of those alps, Moel Siabod, this walk will round the valley, taking in views of the wide sweep of mountains that surround Capel Curig and the Llugwy Valley. There's an optional scramble to Capel's very own pinnacle, Y Pincin, where you can see the five distinctive peaks of Snowdon reflected beautifully below in the twin lakes of Mymbyr.

To the Woods

You continue through those oak woods seen by Pennant, now wonderfully matured, before descending back down to the boisterous river. In front of the Ty'n y Coed Inn they have one of the old London to Holyhead stagecoaches on display. After crossing the river at Pont-Cyfyng you follow its delightful banks for a short while, then go over crag, across pasture and through the woods. You come out by a footbridge on the shores of Llynnau Mymbyr, and again you see Snowdon, maybe still perfectly reflected in glass-like waters. On the other side of the bridge at the Plas y Brenin National Mountain Centre, they're training the next generation of mountaineers.

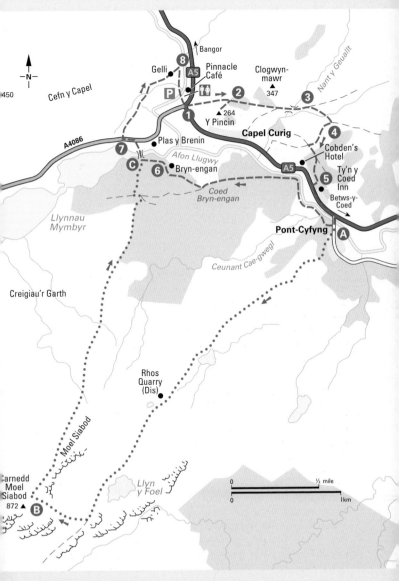

WALK 23 DIRECTIONS

1 The path begins at a ladder stile by the war memorial on the A5 and climbs towards Y Pincin, a large craggy outcrop cloaked in wood and bracken. Go over another stile and keep to the left of the outcrop. Those who want to go to the top should do so from the north-east, where the gradients are easier. It's fun, but take care! You'll need to retrace your steps to the main route.

2 Continue east through woods and across marshy ground, keeping well to the right of the great crags of Clogwyn-mawr. On reaching a couple of ladder stiles, ignore the footpath, right, back down to the road, but maintain your direction across the hillside.

3 Just beyond a footbridge over Nant y Geuallt, leave the main footpath and follow a less well-defined one, with marker posts, across marshy ground. This path veers south-east to cross another stream before coming to a prominent track.

4 Turn right along the track, go over a ladder stile, then at a four-way meeting of paths head left. Follow the path descending into some woods. Take the right-hand fork descending to the road near Ty'n y Coed Inn.

5 Turn left down the road, then right, along the lane over Pont-Cyfyng. Go right again beyond the bridge to follow a footpath that traces the Llugwy to another bridge opposite Cobdens Hotel. Don't cross this time, but scramble left over some rocks before continuing through the woods of Coed Bryn-engan, where the path soon becomes a wide track.

6 After passing the cottage of Bryn-engan, the track comes to the bridge at the head of the Mymbyr lakes. Turn right across it, then go left along the road for a short way.

7 Cross the road to the next ladder stile and take a track straight ahead, soon swinging right to hug the foot of the southern Glyder slopes.

8 When you get beyond Gelli farm turn right to follow the cart track back to the car park.

Climbing Moel Siabod

*A climb to Siabod's rocky summit gives you the best
view of Snowdon.*
See map and information panel for Walk 23

DISTANCE 7 miles (11.3km) **MINIMUM TIME** 4hrs 30min

ASCENT/GRADIENT 2,723ft (830m) ▲▲▲ **LEVEL OF DIFFICULTY** +++

WALK 24 DIRECTIONS
(Walk 23 Option)

Leave Walk 23 at Pont-Cyfyng,
Point **Ⓐ**. Cross the bridge and
walk up the lane to a track on the
right signed 'No Cars or Bikes'.
Follow a signed footpath diversion
then rejoin the now rougher track
by a derelict house.

By now the cone of Moel Siabod
can be seen rising from the stark
low moors that lie ahead. The
track ends, to be replaced by a
prominent path that keeps to the
left of a rocky spur thrown out by
the mountain.

After traversing rough peaty
slopes the path passes a pleasant
unnamed lake before coming to
the derelict Rhos quarries. Beyond
the old workers' barracks it passes
to the left of a deep black quarry
pool and climbs more peaty slopes
to look down on Llyn y Foel,
under the rocky slopes of Siabod.

The footpath becomes
intermittent as it
struggles with the
marshy ground
to the west of the
tarn, but soon
reaches terra
firma on Siabod's
south-east spur.
Be careful not
to miss the right

turn up the rocky spur here, for
the footpath you're on continues
beyond it, only to lose itself on the
mountain's southern slopes.

It's an exhilarating climb on easy
rock, right to the summit of Moel
Siabod, Point **Ⓑ**, and the view
of Snowdon is as good as you'll
get, for you can see the whole of
the Horseshoe and all the major
peaks. Glyder Fach's bristly rocks
and Tryfan's distinctive buttresses
add spice to the view across
Nant Gwryd, while the rolling
Carneddau fill the northern
horizon – here you see all the
3,000ft (914m) peaks at a glance.

From the summit ignore the rocky
ridge top, but stay just to the left
of it on the short grass. Eventually
a faint path rakes north-north-east
down the left side of the spur. The
path becomes more prominent
as you descend towards Plas y
Brenin. Ignore twin ladder stiles
in a fence on your right. Continue
down to heathland beside a forest,
then enter the forest
itself. Meet a forestry
track, turn left, then
right after a few paces
on a path descending
to the Mymbyr lakes

You meet Walk 23 by
the bridge at Plas y
Brenin, Point **Ⓒ**.

Overleaf: Snowdon reflected in Llannau Mymbyr (Walk 24)

Tall Tales and Miners' Trails

Discover Snowdon's inner cwms in a landscape steeped in history and legend.

DISTANCE 5 miles (8km)	**MINIMUM TIME** 3hrs
ASCENT/GRADIENT 1,509ft (460m) ▲▲▲	**LEVEL OF DIFFICULTY** +++

PATHS Engineered paths, 1 stile

LANDSCAPE High mountain corries and tarns

SUGGESTED MAP OS Explorer OL17 Snowdon

START / FINISH Grid reference: SH 647556

DOG FRIENDLINESS Sheep may be met in summer; keep dogs on lead

PARKING Pen-y-pass car park

PUBLIC TOILETS At car park

WALK 25 DIRECTIONS

Tucked beneath the cold hard rocks of Glyder Fawr and Crib Goch, the high Pass of Llanberis would have been an awesome sight for the early traveller. There wasn't a road until 1830, so traders and farmers passing through would have had to take their horse-drawn sledges over the boulder-strewn and boggy ground you still see away from the path.

With the building of the road came an inn, where the weary travellers could stop and rest before resuming their journey towards the coast. The new inn came a poor second in popularity to the Pen-y-Gwryd Inn, a mile (1.6km) back along the road to Capel Curig, until the enterprising Owen Rawson Owen took over in 1900. At about this time tourists were flocking into Snowdonia, including rock climbers like Geoffrey Winthrop Young, who regularly patronised Owen's Gorphwysfa Hotel.

Today, you start your walk on a firmer footing than the traders of the past; treading the slabbed rocks of the Pyg Track. Or should that be the Pig Track? Opinion is divided. If it's the Pig Track, then the name is derived from Bwlch Moch, which in Welsh, means pass of the pig. Pyg would come from the Pen-y-Gwryd, where many of the early travellers started their climb up Snowdon.

From the far right of the car park go through a gap in the wall and follow the path up the rough slopes high above the Pass of Llanberis. The path reaches Bwlch y Moch, a wild pass on the northern ridge of Snowdon's

WHAT TO LOOK OUT FOR

The Snowdon lily, a relic of the glacial period, is a hardy arctic plant that is only found on the rocky ledges of Snowdon and the Glyders. It was discovered in the 17th century by Edward Llwyd, and it's Latin name, *Lloydia serotina*, reflects this. A perennial bulb, this lily has long, narrow leaves and small white flowers that bloom in April and May.

WHILE YOU'RE THERE

The Electric Mountain in Llanberis is the starting point for tours around the Dinorwig Power Station, a hydroelectric scheme where the main plant is housed beneath the mountain. The head of water is provided by a reservoir connected to the station by pipelines driven through the heart of Elidr Fawr.

horseshoe. From here you look down into the cavernous Cwm Dyli and its huge lake, Llyn Llydaw. Snowdon's highest peak, Yr Wyddfa peeps over the shoulder of Crib Goch at the head of the cwm, but for now centre stage is taken by the immense cliffs that rise from the shores of Llyn Llydaw to the twin summits of Y Lliwedd. According to legend, King Arthur was slain at the nearby Bwlch y Saethau (pass of the arrows) after a battle with his mortal enemy, Sir Mordred. While Arthur's body was taken down the mountainside, many of his Knights of the Round Table, feeling that their King would return, retreated to a cave where they still wait…

Ignoring the smaller path to the summit of Crib Goch, stay with the wide path that rounds the corner to traverse Crib Goch's lower slopes. The path climbs high above Llyn Llydaw. On the skyline above, you may just about make out walkers crossing the knife-edged ridges of Crib Goch and Garnedd Ugain.

The path climbs to overlook Glaslyn, a circular tarn whose blue-green waters are cradled in spectacular surroundings beneath the pyramid of dark cliffs that form Yr Wyddfa. Legend has this lake as bottomless, and home to Afanc, a fearsome monster who

was thrown into its depths after gorging himself on too many damsels in distress – a nice story, but nobody's seen him since.

When you're above the western shores of Glaslyn, watch out for the path climbing from the left. Follow this rougher path down scree slopes to the lakeshores.

Here you pick up the Miners' Track, a wide flinted road that traces Glaslyn's shoreline, past the stark remains of the Brittania Copper Mines, founded in the 18th century. Originally the slate had to be hauled up the mountainside to Bwlch Glas, then taken down the other side on horse-drawn sledges to Rhyd Ddu where it continued by horse and cart to Caernarfon. However, the building of the Miners' Track and the causeway across Llyn Llydaw in 1853 made it possible for the ore carts to be taken to Pen-y-pass. The mine closed in 1926.

The track descends past the waterfalls of Glaslyn's outflow and down to the shores of Llyn Llydaw, where it passes the ruins of the ore-crushing mill belonging to the Brittania Mine. The route crosses the lake, using the previously mentioned causeway, then rounds a rocky knoll to come upon Llyn Teyrn, another circular tarn. There's a fine view of the valley of Nantgwynant and Moel Siabod behind it.

Beyond Llyn Teyrn the track swings left to head northwards, back to the car park.

WHERE TO EAT AND DRINK

There's the Gorphwysfa Café if you want a snack meal and a drink. If you want a tasty pub meal, try the Vaynol Arms in Nant Peris.

Snowdon the Long Way

*A route that takes its time on one of
Snowdon's seldom-trod ridges.*

DISTANCE *10 miles (16.1km)*   MINIMUM TIME *6hrs 30min*

ASCENT/GRADIENT *3,839ft (1,170m)* ▲▲▲ LEVEL OF DIFFICULTY +++

PATHS *Well-defined paths and tracks, 1 stile*

LANDSCAPE *High mountain cwms and tarns*

SUGGESTED MAP *OS Explorer OL17 Snowdon*

START / FINISH *Grid reference: SH 577604*

DOG FRIENDLINESS *Sheep, trains and crags: best on lead throughout*

PARKING *Several car parks throughout Llanberis*

PUBLIC TOILETS *Just off High Street, south of tourist information centre*

Llanberis is a slate town, you can see that by looking across Llyn Padarn to the dismal purple-grey terraces built into the mountainside. However it's easy to look the other way, to where Snowdon reigns supreme in the skies.

In Victorian times the interest in mountains was in its infancy. Being Wales' highest peak, attention was centred on Snowdon and the village at its foot. The Snowdon Mountain Railway was built, and opened in 1896 with a fanfare of publicity. Unfortunately, on the first day, a descending train ran out of control and was derailed round a bend, before tumbling down steep slopes. One passenger who jumped from a falling carriage was killed. Since then the steam engines on the rack-and-pinion railway have chugged up the mountain pushing their red and cream carriages for 4.5 miles (7.2km) to the summit without incident. Though a few resent the trains' presence, most walkers are comforted by the whistles that pierce the mountain mists or the plumes of smoke billowing into a blue sky.

The route through the Arddu Valley is a pleasing and peaceful way into the hills. In the early stages you'll ease by the shaly flanks of Moel Eilio before climbing to a dark pass on the Eilio–Snowdon ridge. The mile-long (1.6km) route from the pass to Moel Cynghorion is a bit of a grind, but the summit reveals your prize – a headlong view of Clogwyn Du'r Arddu's black cliffs and several remote tarns basking in two cwms below.

The route joins the Snowdon Ranger Path and zig-zags up Cloggy's rocky arm to Bwlch Glas, where you meet the crowds. Here, you gaze into Cwm Dyli, where the blue-green lakes of Glaslyn and Llydaw lie beneath the ridges of Garnedd Ugain, Crib Goch, and Y Lliwedd.

Now those crowds will lead you alongside the railway to gain the pile of rocks capping Snowdon's highest summit, Yr Wyddfa, where the ugly old summit buildings have been replaced with a new visitor centre, open from summer 2008 Snowdon's summit panorama is stunning with several peaks in view: you can see half of Wales laid out at your feet. Look further to the distant misty mountains in Ireland and the Isle of Man stretching across the horizon. Our way down Snowdon is easier than the way up: you could even catch the train if you had a mind to. The Llanberis Path is long but it descends in gentle gradients across bare hillsides above the rugged fields of the Arddu Valley.

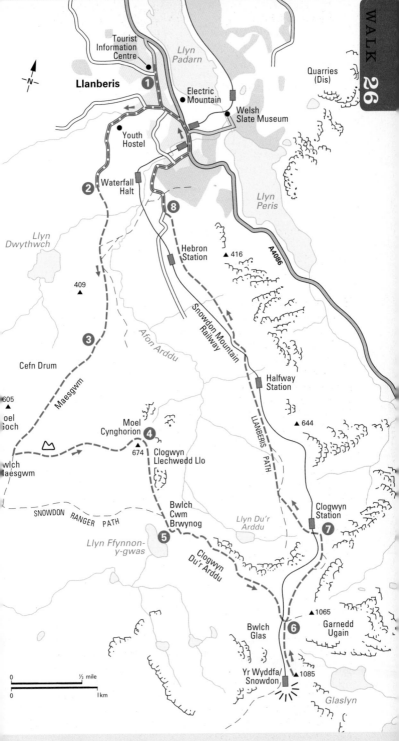

WALK 26 DIRECTIONS

1 From the tourist information centre in the heart of Llanberis, head south along the High Street (Stryd Fawr) before turning right up Capel Coch Road. Go straight ahead at a junction, where the road changes its name to Stryd Ceunant, and follow the road past the youth hostel. The road winds and climbs towards Braich y Foel, the north-east spur of Moel Eilio.

2 Where the tarmac ends at the foot of Moel Eilio, continue along the track, which swings left (south-east) into the wild cwm of the Afon Arddu. On the other side of the cwm you'll see the trains of the Snowdon Mountain Railway, puffing up and down the line.

3 On reaching the base of Foel Goch's northern spur, Cefn Drum, the track swings right into Maesgwm and climbs to a pass, Bwlch Maesgwm, between Foel Goch and Moel Cynghorion. Go through the gate here, then turn left and follow the route for the steep climb by the fence and up the latter-mentioned peak.

4 From Cynghorion's summit the route descends along the top of the cliffs of Clogwyn Llechwedd Llo to another pass, Bwlch Cwm Brwynog, which overlooks the small reservoir of Llyn Ffynnon-y-gwas. Here you join the Snowdon Ranger Path.

WHAT TO LOOK OUT FOR

Yr Wyddfa means the grave. The pile of stones on the summit is supposedly the grave of giant Rhita Gawr, who attempted to rob King Arthur of his beard. Arthur decapitated Rhita with his sword and the giant's head was left where it fell.

5 Follow the zig-zag route up Clogwyn Du'r Arddu, whose cliffs, on the left, plummet to a little tarn, Llyn Du'r Arddu, which sits uneasily in a dark stony cwm. Near the top the wide path veers right, away from the edge, meets the Snowdon Mountain Railway, and follows the line to the monolith at Bwlch Glas. Here you are met by both the Llanberis Path and the Pyg Track and look down on the huge cwms of Glaslyn and Llyn Llydaw.

WHILE YOU'RE THERE

The Welsh Slate Museum by the lake gives an insight into the story of slate. There is a 3D show and demonstrations by craftspeople.

6 The path now follows the line of the railway to the summit. Retrace your steps to Bwlch Glas, but this time follow the wide Llanberis Path traversing the western slopes of Garnedd Ugain and above the railway. (Make sure you don't mistake this for the higher ridge path to Garnedd Ugain's summit.)

WHERE TO EAT AND DRINK

Pete's Eats on the High Street in Llanberis is one of the best chippies in the world.

7 Near Clogwyn Station you come to Cwm Hetiau, where cliffs fall away into the chasm of the Pass of Llanberis. The path goes under the railway and below Clogwyn Station before recrossing the line near Halfway Station.

8 The path meets a lane beyond Hebron, and this descends back into Llanberis near the Royal Victoria Hotel. Turn left along the main road, then take the left fork, High Street, to get back to the car.

In the Country of Lloyd George

Explore the countryside and coastal haunts of the last Liberal Prime Minister.

DISTANCE 6 miles (9.7km)   MINIMUM TIME 4hrs

ASCENT/GRADIENT 300ft (91m) ▲▲▲   LEVEL OF DIFFICULTY ✚✚✚

PATHS Generally well-defined paths and tracks, 4 stiles

LANDSCAPE Riverside woodland, fields, town streets, coastline

SUGGESTED MAP OS Explorer 254 Lleyn Peninsula East

START / FINISH Grid reference: SH 476383

DOG FRIENDLINESS Dogs can run free in riverside woods and on coast

PARKING Large car park at east end of village

PUBLIC TOILETS Near museum at Llanystumdwy and at Criccieth

NOTE Small section of coast path engulfed by highest tides. Make sure you know times of tides before setting off

'As a man of action, resource and creative energy he stood, when at his zenith, without rival... He was the greatest Welshman which that unconquerable race has produced since the age of the Tudors... and those who come after us will find the pillars of his life's toil upstanding, massive and indestructible'

Winston Churchill, 1945
A Parliamentary tribute to David Lloyd George

David Lloyd George (1863–1945) came from modest beginnings in Llanystumdwy. This village on the banks of the Dwyfor is separated from the coast by half a mile (800m) of fields and coastal marshes. When you're barely out of the car park, you'll pass Highgate, his boyhood home, and the Lloyd George Museum. In the woods at the start of the walk you will come across the grave and a memorial to this last Liberal Prime Minister of Great Britain. It's a spot where he loved to sit.

Controversial Life

That Lloyd George was a great man is not in dispute, but his life was not without controversy. Although he was one of the early pioneers of the Welfare State and led Britain to eventual victory in World War One, he was also linked with several dubious private moneymaking deals and gained a, perhaps unfair, reputation for allowing peerages to be awarded to wealthy political benefactors. A flamboyant, larger-than-life man Lloyd George just did not fit in with his rather stuffy Edwardian contemporaries. He is reputed to have been a womaniser, and at one time he had a wife in Criccieth and a mistress, his parliamentary secretary, whom he later married, in London.

Leaving things historical for a while, the walk through the woodland by the Dwyfor riverside is as good as woodland walking gets. The Dwyfor's crystal clear waters chatter to the rocks below and in spring the forest floor is carpeted with primroses, bluebells, garlic and wood anemones. So far we've been heading away

79

from Criccieth and the coast, but soon the route takes us back across fields into Criccieth, a town with history in two episodes.

The Great Castle

Criccieth Castle stands on a huge volcanic crag that juts out into Tremadog Bay. It's synonymous with Edward I's 'iron ring' but, unlike the others, there was already a Welsh castle on the spot – Edward only had to annexe and enlarge it. The twin-towered gatehouse is believed to have been built by Llewelyn the Great, around 1240, some 40 years before Edward took it off him. Yet it was a Welshman who was responsible for the castle's downfall! In 1404 Owain Glyndwr captured it, then burnt it to the ground.

Victorian Expansion

Despite its one-time strategic importance, Criccieth stayed a small fishing port until the Victorians penchant for sun and sand saw it grow to today's proportions. You'll pass the rows of Victorian terraces on the way to the rugged coastal path which takes you by the sand and pebble beach back to the Dwyfor and David Lloyd George's village.

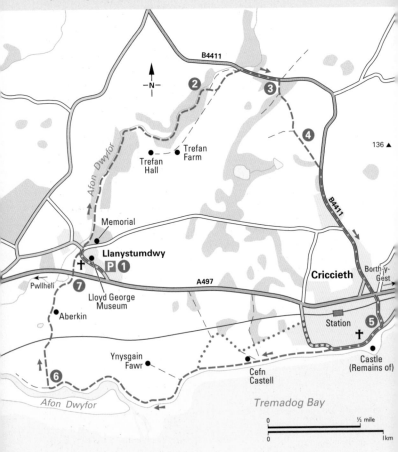

LLANYSTUMDWY

WALK 27 DIRECTIONS

1 Turn right out of the car park and go through Llanystumdwy village, past the museum to the bridge over the Afon Dwyfor. Turn right along the lane, then follow the footpath on the left past the memorial and down to the wooded river banks.

2 After 1.5 miles (2.4km) the path turns right, then goes under a stone archway to meet a tarred drive. Turn left along this, carry on to the B4411 and turn right.

3 After about 500yds (457m), turn right down an enclosed drive. As another drive merges from the left, turn half left along a path shaded by rhododendrons. After a few paces, go though the kissing gate, then cross the field guided by a fence on the left. Through another kissing gate the path veers half right, following a fence which is now on the right.

4 Beyond another gate the now sketchy route cuts diagonally (south-east) across two fields to rejoin the B4411, a mile (1.6km) or so north of Criccieth. Follow the B4411 into town. Keep straight on at the crossroads, and bear left after the level crossing to reach the promenade.

5 Follow the coast road past the castle and continue until it turns firmly inland. From here, tide permitting, simply follow

the coast path or walk along the sands. Otherwise, follow the road to a bridleway on the left. Go past Muriau and then to the right of Ty Cerrig. Cross a track and a field then turn right on a green track, nearly to the railway. Head left, back to the coast east of Ynysgain Fawr. Follow the coast path west through coastal grasslands and gorse scrub to the estuary of the Dwyfor and some crumbled concrete sea defences.

6 At a metal kissing gate, waymarks point inland. Follow these, with the fence on your right. The route becomes a farm track that cuts under the railway and passes through the yard of Aberkin farm before reaching the main road.

7 Cross the main road with care and go through the gate on the opposite side. A short path leads to an unsurfaced lane, which in turn leads to the village centre. Turn right for the car park.

In the Beautiful Ceiriog Valley

Discover an earthly heaven in one of ancient Clwyd's truly green and pleasant valleys.

> DISTANCE *3.75 miles (6km)*   MINIMUM TIME *2hrs 30min*
> ASCENT/GRADIENT *853ft (260m)* ▲▲▲   LEVEL OF DIFFICULTY +++
> PATHS *Sketchy paths and farm tracks, 4 stiles*
> LANDSCAPE *Pastoral hillscapes and river scenery*
> SUGGESTED MAP *OS Explorer 255 Llangollen & Berwyn*
> START / FINISH *Grid reference: SJ 157328*
> DOG FRIENDLINESS *Whole walk through sheep country, keep dogs on lead*
> PARKING *Roadside parking in village*
> PUBLIC TOILETS *At village hall*

David Lloyd George, the last Liberal Party Prime Minister of Britain, described the Ceiriog Valley as 'a piece of heaven that has fallen to earth'. For 18 miles (29km), from its source on the slopes of Mount Fferna in the Berwyns to its meeting with the Dee, the beautiful Afon Ceiriog meanders through oak woods, rocky hillsides and fertile cattle pastures. Yet in 1923 city planners wanted to turn this little piece of heaven into a huge reservoir. If these planners had won the day, the locals living within an area of 13,600 acres (5,508ha) would have been evicted from their homes. Fortunately Parliament denied their whims.

While Glyn Ceiriog is the largest village, Llanarmon Dyffryn Ceiriog is the most beautiful. Lying by the confluence of the Ceiriog and a tributary, the Gwrachen, it was a natural fording place for drovers bound for the markets of England. You'll be using some of their old roads on Walks 28 and 29. The village and its church take their name from the 5th-century missionary, St Garmon. The present church is early Victorian and, unusually, has two pulpits. A mound in the churchyard, known as Tomen Garmon, is believed to be a Bronze Age burial mound and the place where the missionary preached.

A Pastoral Idyll

The walk begins behind the church, and follows pretty pastures above the Ceiriog and woods full of bluebells before coming to the old Mill (Y Felin) at Tregeiriog. In the 19th century, author George Borrow revelled in the pastoral nature of this landscape. He spent hours standing on the bridge, watching pigs foraging by the river bank while the old Mill's waterwheel slowly turned; a scene he said that 'was well-suited to the brushes of two or three of the old Dutch painters'.

From the old Mill the route climbs on one of those drovers' roads on to the small hills overlooking the valley. You can see many a mile of rolling green hills as a winding green track climbs towards some crags on the horizon. Here you enter a wilder world of rushy moorland with views down the valleys of Nant y Glôg and the Gwrachen. After tramping through the bracken of the high hillside you join another green road which accompanies the Gwrachen. By now you may be following the footsteps of Owain Glyndwr, 15th-century Prince of Wales, who would have passed through Llanarmon when travelling between his residences at Sycharth and Glyndyfrdwy in the Dee Valley.

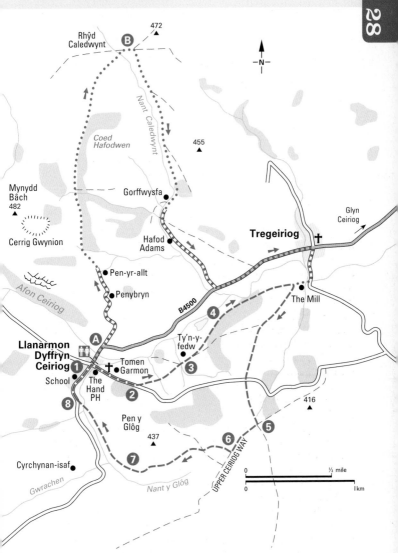

WALK 28 DIRECTIONS

❶ From The Hand, take the eastbound lane past the church and uphill with a conifer plantation on the right and the pastures of the Ceiriog below left.

❷ At the far end of the plantation leave the road for a farm track on the left. This ends at a barn. Keep to the right of the barn and aim for a gate beyond it. Through the gate maintain your direction, over the shoulder of a grassy knoll, then aim for a stile in a fence ahead. Beyond this, cross another field down to a gate, through which mount a stile on the right.

3 Bear left, crossing two streamlets to join a track past Ty'n-y-fedw farm. Don't go through the gate, but follow a grass path right beside the fence, shortly entering a wood

4 Keep ahead to the far end of the woods. Emerging into a field, a grass trod curves round to a gate at the top corner. Turn right along a rising farm track, ignoring junctions to reach a lane. Next cross to the ongoing track opposite, which climbs on through the high pastures.

5 At a crossroads, turn right along a green track – part of the Upper Ceiriog Way. This heads south-west towards the green hill known as Cefn-Hîr-fynydd

6 After about 300yds (274m) leave this track through a gate on the right. If you head west by the right edge of the rushy area and towards Pen y Glôg's sparse crags, it will be easy to find the small stile in the next fence, then the wooden gate on the left soon afterwards. Through the gate head downhill with a faint sheep path past a low clump of rocks on the

left, and aiming for the distant farm of Cyrchynan-isaf.

7 Lower down, a developing grassy track runs on through the valley of Nant y Glôg contouring the lower slopes of Pen y Glôg, and eventually reaching a gate.

8 After swinging right with the lively stream the track terminates by a lane to the south of Llanarmon Dyffryn Ceiriog. Follow the lane past several attractive cottages and the village school to arrive by the Hand hotel in the village square.

On to the Moors

A longer loop takes you out to Ceiriog's moorlands fringe.
See map and information panel for Walk 28

DISTANCE 7 miles (11.3km) **MINIMUM TIME** 4hrs

ASCENT/GRADIENT 1,394ft (425m) ▲▲▲ **LEVEL OF DIFFICULTY** ✦✦✦

WALK 29 DIRECTIONS
(Walk 28 option)

This route discovers the north side of the Ceiriog, where you get more of a taste of the wild heather moors and glimpses of the higher Berwyn peaks. It follows old drovers' routes to the ford of the Caledwynt before visiting the hamlet of Tregeiriog.

Starting at the Hand hotel in the centre of the village, head north-east past the West Arms and the village hall before going over the Ceiriog bridge, Point **A**. As the road bends right, leave it for a narrow lane climbing steeply up the hillside. You'll pass the whitewashed farm of Penybryn, which was home to the Welsh poet, John 'Ceiriog' Hughes, who won in the National Eisteddfod in 1858. There's a memorial stone on the road edge.

The tarmac ends at the next farm, Pen-yr-allt, from where there's an easy stroll along a stony track past several copses of pine and spruce. To the left on Mynydd Bâch are the remains of an old fort known as Cerrig Gwynion. Although at one time this was believed to be Roman, historians now believe it to be an Iron Age settlement.

Beyond the highest of the plantations, Coed Hafodwen, the track enters rough moorland. It becomes rutted and gradually swings north-east with some gaunt pine trees dominant on the skyline ahead. It fords a stream at Rhyd Caledwynt, Point **B**, before climbing out on to the far bank. After 100yds (91m), as a fence closes from the left, swing off right on a vague grass track that curves above the deepening valley. Soon becoming more pronounced, it drops through a gate, beyond which keep with the lower track at successive forks.

Follow this all the way down the valley. At Gorffwsyfa, the tarmac reappears, the lane dropping to Hafod Adams. The farmhouse is one of the oldest longhouses of the region and used to be a resting place for monks travelling to Valle Crucis Abbey (see Walk 21). Keep ahead past a junction to meet the main valley road. Turn left into Tregeiriog village, and then right at the phone box to cross the Afon Ceiriog.

Just beyond the bridge, turn right past The Mill and go through a gate which gives access to a farm lane. This runs parallel to the river at first, but soon climbs left to join Walk 28 to Pen y Glôg.

Chirk Castle and Ceiriog's Aqueduct and Viaduct

See one of Edward I's best 'iron ring' castles and Thomas Telford's magnificent aqueduct.

DISTANCE 6 miles (9.7km) **MINIMUM TIME** 3hrs 30min

ASCENT/GRADIENT 1,115ft (340m) ▲▲▲ **LEVEL OF DIFFICULTY** ✦✦✦

PATHS Well-defined woodland paths and tracks, 15 stiles

LANDSCAPE Limestone hillside and mixed woodland

SUGGESTED MAP OS Explorer 240 Oswestry

START / FINISH Grid reference: SJ 291371 (on Explorer 255)

DOG FRIENDLINESS Dogs should be on lead, except by canal

PARKING Small car park by canal at Chirk Bank

PUBLIC TOILETS None en route

NOTE Route through Chirk Estate only open between April and end of September. At other times take detour on quiet lanes rounding New Hall and its reservoir to Tyn-y-groes

---

WALK 30 DIRECTIONS

Chirk is a former coal mining community, sited high on a hillside that separates the River Dee from the Ceiriog. It's in Wales, just, though if you wander any distance at all, you'll be stepping in and out of Shropshire too.

The walk starts at Chirk Bank, just over the border with England, following the tow path of the Llangollen branch of the Shropshire Union Canal. Chocolate-box cottages with rose gardens and hollyhocks line the tow path before you arrive at the deep chasm of the Ceiriog Valley, which has to be crossed. Engineer Thomas Telford's solution was the ten-arched aqueduct, of 1801, to convey the canal more than 70ft (21m) above the valley bottom. To your left is Henry Robertson's even taller viaduct, built in 1840 to carry the railway. Both canal

and railway were built to convey the coal from these once thriving Flintshire coalfields.

After crossing the aqueduct the footpath climbs to the B4500 on the outskirts of Chirk. Turn left for a few paces, then right along Station Road. Turn left at the railway station, following a road to some magnificent wrought-iron gates, built for the Chirk Estate in 1721 by the Davies Brothers of Bersham.

Swing right with the road, but soon turn off left through a gate on to the National Trust's Chirk Estate (if the Estate is closed

---

WHERE TO EAT AND DRINK

The Hand hotel at Chirk is a large 19th-century coaching house, which does rather tasty Sunday roasts. It is child friendly and reasonably priced.

continue on the road to Tyn-y-groes) and trace a fence on the left to another gate. Here you angle a right, across the fields in the direction of the first of many white-topped waymarking posts. The estate's grounds are very spacious, and there's over a mile (1.6km) of walking across lawn-like fields, scattered with fine mature oak trees. Once through another kissing gate, trace a fence on the left westwards to meet a junction of drives. Take the one ahead towards the car park.

The castle was built in 1310 by Edward I's Justice of Wales, Roger Mortimer, and replaced the 11th-century wooden motte-and-bailey castle south of the town. The walls of the castle have now been decorated by scores of mullioned windows, hiding the stark repressive face those powerful circular towers once issued.

Chirk Castle has been continuously inhabited ever since, and by the Myddleton Family from 1595. The Myddleton's heraldic icon 'the bloody red hand' can be seen on their coat of arms and on the signs of many a local pub.

Go right past Home Farm and the edge of the car park to continue on a rough track across fields to the road corner at Tyn-y-groes.

WHILE YOU'RE THERE

You must see the castle when you're out of your boots. Besides having attractive gardens, the castle interior includes exquisite state rooms with Adams-style furniture, tapestries and fine portraits. Maintained by the National Trust, it is open to the public between Easter and October, Wednesday to Sunday (also Tuesday in July and August) and bank holidays.

Immediately past a cottage, turn left over a stile. Head south-west across successive pastures passing left of Mars Wood. Descend steeply to a final stile and then go left along a banked cart track, which drops past two farms.

WHAT TO LOOK OUT FOR

Just by the Home Farm entrance you'll notice a line of raised ground. This is the remains of Offa's Dyke, a coast-to-coast earthwork built for the Anglo-Saxon King Offa, in the 8th century, to keep the troublesome Welsh warlords from making forays into England.

Keep ahead beyond Ty Brickly and then fork right along a narrow tarred lane down to the B4500 at Castle Mill.

Cross the B4500 to follow the lane going over the bridge across the Ceiriog to Brnygarth. Turn left along the road at the other side, passing the old schoolhouse before turning left down a lane that descends past several cottages towards the river. Beyond the last cottage, continue on a descending gated path. Bear right into Pentre Wood, where the path joins the River Ceiriog. Carry on in a meadow, finally emerging on to a lane. Go left to Pont Faen.

Just before a sharp right bend, take a path on the left through woods. Emerging over a stile, turn left at the edge of a couple of fields. Reaching the railway line, carefully cross and keep going beside another pasture. Leaving at the far side, cross to a ginnel opposite between houses, which comes out at Chirk Bank. Go left back to the car park.

Cadair Berwyn and Pistyll Rhaeadr

A demanding, but short walk brings magnificent views and a visit to spectacular falls.

WALK 31

DISTANCE *5 miles (8km)* MINIMUM TIME *3hrs*

ASCENT/GRADIENT *1,870ft (570m)* ▲▲▲ LEVEL OF DIFFICULTY +++

PATHS *Well-defined paths and tracks, 7 stiles*

LANDSCAPE *Mountain and moorland*

SUGGESTED MAP *OS Explorer 255 Llangollen & Berwyn*

START / FINISH *Grid reference: SJ 076293*

DOG FRIENDLINESS *Sheep usually present: dogs should be on lead*

PARKING *Car park 220yds (201m) before Tan-y-pistyll farm/café, where there's another pay car park*

PUBLIC TOILETS *At Tan-y-pistyll pay car park*

'What shall I liken it to? I scarcely know, unless to an immense skein of silk agitated and disturbed by tempestuous blasts, or to the long tail of a grey courser at furious speed'

This is how author, George Borrow saw the thunderous falls of Pistyll Rhaeadr in his travels in *Wild Wales* (1862). But Borrow ignored the beautiful mountain valley to the right of the falls, instead choosing to wander off south in search of the site of Owain Glyndwr's castle at Sycharth. We'll not make that same mistake, for that valley, fringed by crag and dappled with heather and bracken, leads to Llyn Lluncaws. Here's a dramatic scene – a wild Welsh cwm in which the lake lies dark and sombre among frazzled heather that can't quite take hold and tussocky moor grass that fills in the extra spaces.

Up in the Gods

A peat and slate path beats a tortuous route by the cwm's cliff edge up on to the ridge, and you discover why you came up here in the first place. You find yourself up in the gods, looking over a stage where there's a cast of thousands. At the front, the green cloaked Dee Valley weaves its way though the heather hills of Llangollen and the jagged Aran mountains towards the chorus line, where Cadair Idris, the Rhinogs, and Snowdon parade themselves aloof and often with their heads in the clouds. In the alternative theatre at your back, the Tanat Valley scenery of fields and hedges gives way to the little blue hills of Cheshire and Shropshire in England. The Berwyns are one of the few places in Wales where the cloudberry grows. These shrubs, not unlike a bramble but lacking thorns, cling closely to the ground. You'll have to be up early to get to the sparse fruits first. They belong to the blackberry family but are orange and taste like raspberries.

Cadair Berwyn

At one time everybody assumed that Moel Sych and Cadair Berwyn were, at 2,713ft (827m), jointly the highest Berwyns – the OS maps that walkers used said so. But everyone who walked the Berwyns looked quizzically across to that little rock peak forming Cadair Berwyn's south summit – it seemed higher. When the OS checked their large scale maps they found that, at 2,723ft (830m), it indeed was the 'tops'.

No Warning

Moel Sych is just a broad flat top, with a cairn for you to pat on your way down to the falls. Amid pretty mixed woodland the peaceful Afon Disgynfa trickles playfully over rocks then, without warning, tumbles off the end of the world. Walkers who have made the ascent look on, amazed, then take the gentler zig-zag route down to the same place. Back in Tan-y-pistyll the café awaits!

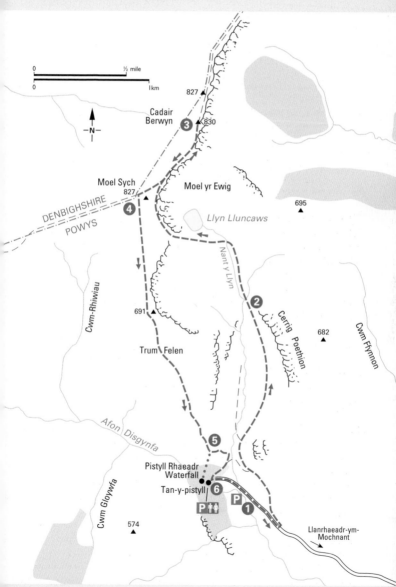

WALK 31

WALK 31 DIRECTIONS

❶ From the more easterly, and the smaller, of the two car parks turn right along the road for about 400yds (366m), then turn sharp left to follow a wide grassy track that climbs north-west to enter the cwm of Nant y Llyn. At an obvious fork keep right on a rising track heading north towards the crags of Cerrig Poethion.

❷ The track degenerates into a path that traverses hillsides scattered with gorse. Higher up it crosses two streams before reaching Llyn Lluncaws in the moss and heather cwm. Now the path climbs south of the lake and up a shale and grass spur to the left of Moel Sych's crags. Follow the path along the edge of the crags on the right to reach the col between Moel Sych and Cadair Berwyn. From here climb to the rocky south top of the latter peak. The onward trip to the trig point on Cadair Berwyn's lower north summit is straightforward but offers no advantages as a viewpoint.

❸ From the south top retrace your footsteps to the col, but this time instead of tracing the cliff edge you now follow the ridge fence to the cairn on Moel Sych summit plateau, crossing a stile just before reaching it.

❹ Recross the stile and turn right (south) to follow the fence down a wide, peaty spur cloaked with moor grass, mosses and a little heather. Over a slight rise, the path descends again to a stile (wobbly when checked) before dropping into the high moorland cwm of the Disgynfa, where the path is met by a stony track that climbs from the base of the falls.

❺ If you want to make a there-and-back detour to the top of the falls, ignore the stony track,

and instead go through a gate into the forest and follow the path to the river. If not, descend along the previously mentioned track, which zig-zags down before turning right to head for the Tan-y-pistyll complex. There's a path to the bottom of the falls starting from the café. It leads to a footbridge across the Afon Rhaeadr for the best views.

❻ From the café it's a short walk along the road to the car park.

Tackling the Knight

Tackle this exhilarating climb to the top of one of Snowdonia's best peaks.

DISTANCE *6.5 miles (10.4km)* **MINIMUM TIME** *4hrs 30min*

ASCENT/GRADIENT *2,297ft (700m)* ▲▲▲ **LEVEL OF DIFFICULTY** +++

PATHS *Mostly well-defined, but sketchy by Bwlch y Battel, 9 stiles*

LANDSCAPE *High pastureland giving way to rocky mountain ridges*

SUGGESTED MAP *OS Explorer OL17 Snowdon*

START / FINISH *Grid reference: SH 634485*

DOG FRIENDLINESS *Sheep high on ridges in summer so dogs to be on lead*

PARKING *Parking area near Gelli-Iago*

PUBLIC TOILETS *At car park at Nantmor, south of Pass of Aberglaslyn*

Seen from below in the valley of the Glaslyn, Cnicht is a splendid pyramid of rock. It has often been described as the Matterhorn of Wales, though it is perhaps more of an Eiger. Cnicht, which means the knight, is a little bit of a pretender though. Seen from any other angle its rock face is no more than the end of a long ridge radiating from the main Moelwyn–Siabod range.

Splendid Cnicht

The most popular route to Cnicht begins from Croesor, but perhaps the most interesting begins from Gelli-Iago in the partially wooded rugged foothills of the Nanmor valley. At the start a narrow path takes you up by the side of a boisterous stream with little waterfalls overhung with rowan trees. You come to a wild rushy hollow beneath Cnicht's sides. The scenery turns more sombre, especially if the mountains hide behind grey clag. Many birds frequent this area, including the little wren, which feeds on insects found in crevices and screes. It's hard to believe something so small can make so much noise, but this low-flying chestnut-coloured bird can startle you with its 'churring'. The final rock steps up Cnicht's 'nose' are exciting, though not enough to be frightening. Below, the cavernous Cwm Croesor disappears towards the Glaslyn Estuary and the Porthmadog horizon.

Sparkling Tarns

Cnicht has two tops, but the nearer one is the higher. The grassy ridge is a delight to walk, and wherever you look you see a sparkling tarn. One, Llyn Cwm-y-foel is a particularly fine one, tucked beneath the shadowy eastern flanks of Cnicht and precariously perched at the very edge of Cwm Croesor. Many of these tarns are breeding grounds for the sandpiper, a small wading bird with sandy brown head and wings and a white throat.

It all seems so quiet now, but in the 19th century the whole area of Croesor and Bwlch y Rhosydd, below, would have echoed to the sound of quarry railways and mining explosions. Slowly the spoil heaps are being swallowed by creeping mosses and grasses as the mountains recover.

CNICHT

The biggest lake you'll see is Llyn yr Adar (lake of the birds), which has an island in the middle. The birds referred to are gulls, and occasionally there are thousands of them – that's because there are trout in the waters. Beyond Llyn yr Adar the route descends to Llyn Llagi, a quite round lake backing on to precipitous cliffs. A waterfall, the outlet stream from Llyn yr Adar, tumbles down them. Always on this descent route, there's Snowdon glowering across the valley, getting higher and higher in the sky as the path slinks down to the valley.

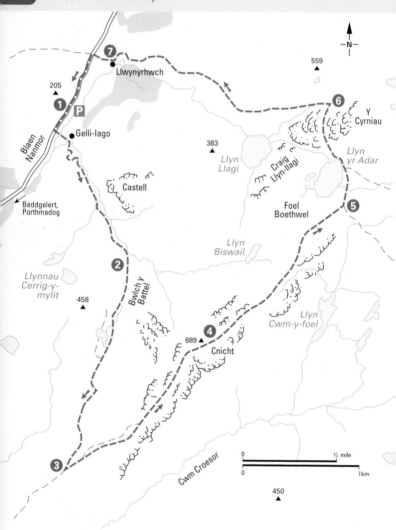

WALK 32 DIRECTIONS

❶ Walk south along the road then turn left along the track to Gelli-Iago (Nantmor Mountain Centre). Go through the gate to the left of the house then round right behind it to a footbridge. A stony path now winds up the hillside, with the stream on the left and Cnicht appearing on the horizon ahead.

2 After a more level stretch, the path veers right and climbs to a ladder stile and the wild pass of Bwlch y Battel. The path peters out, but a marshy passage between high rocky hillsides keeps you on the straight and narrow. Descend towards a tarn and pass above and left of it. Descend by its outlet stream through a narrow valley to a marshy hollow. Bear right on a clearer path and descend a little more to meet a broader path, the main Croesor to Cnicht route

3 Double back to the left on the main path and climb on to the narrowing south ridge of Cnicht, which leads you unerringly to the summit.

4 Continue north-east, overlooking Llyn Biswail on the left and Llyn Cwm-y-foel on the right, to reach the col overlooking a large tarn, Llyn yr Adar.

5 Descend left to traverse the marshy grasslands east of the tarn. The path veers leftward beyond the northern shores before swinging right again to cross a low

notch and then follow a grassy shelf in the rocks of Y Cyrniau. Descend into a bouldery hollow.

6 Follow the stream down, ignoring a small path to the right, until the main path becomes clearer, overlooking Llyn Llagi. Follow the path down over rough moorland and pasture, staying roughly parallel to the outlet stream of the llyn. Finally descend, closer to the stream, to a stile just above Llwynyrhwch farm, with its tall pine tree.

7 Pass in front of the farm then go diagonally right across fields to a cottage. Go straight over the rise to the road and turn left, back to the car park.

There's Copper in Them There Hills

A walk up to the old copper mines of Mynydd Sygyn and through the spectacular Pass of Aberglaslyn.

DISTANCE 4 miles (6.4km) MINIMUM TIME 2hrs 30min

ASCENT/GRADIENT 1,181ft (360m) ▲▲▲ LEVEL OF DIFFICULTY +++

PATHS *Well-maintained paths and tracks (see note below), 2 stiles*

LANDSCAPE *Rocky hills and river gorge*

SUGGESTED MAP *OS Explorer OL17 Snowdon*

START / FINISH *Grid reference: SH 597462*

DOG FRIENDLINESS *Dogs should be on lead at all times*

PARKING *National Trust pay car park, Aberglaslyn*

PUBLIC TOILETS *At car park*

NOTE *Short section of riverside path in Aberglaslyn gorge is difficult and requires use of handholds*

This route heads for the rugged hills forming one side of the great Aberglaslyn gorge that has graced many a postcard and book jacket. At the back of the car park you pass under a railway bridge that belonged to the Welsh Highland Railway and pass the site of an old crushing plant. Here, copper ore from the mountain would have been prepared for shipment, using the railway.

Cwm Bychan

Beyond the plant, the path follows a playful stream and climbs steadily through the lonely Cwm Bychan. Here, beneath splintered, craggy mountains patched with heather and bracken, you come across a line of rusting gantries. They're part of an old aerial ropeway, built to carry ore down to the crushing mill. Mining had taken place hereabouts since Roman times, but after World War One the extraction became uneconomical. In 1922 the mines closed.

Continuing to the col above, the route comes to a huge area of mining spoil and a meeting of routes. Ours turns south, and soon we're following a rugged rocky path zig-zagging down to a grassy basin below before continuing along a craggy ridge. Here the ground drops away steeply into the valley of the Afon Glaslyn. If it's early summer the scene will be emblazoned by the vivid pink blooms of rhododendrons, which smother the hillside. Hundreds of feet below lie the roof tops of Beddgelert and what lies in-between is a glorious little path twisting through those rhododendrons and the rocks into the village. If you get that feeling of déjà vu the hillsides around here were used for the setting of the Chinese village in *The Inn of the Sixth Happiness* (1958), starring Ingrid Bergman.

Beddgelert is a pretty village with a fine two-arched bridge spanning the Glaslyn and a handful of busy craft shops and cafés, which throng with visitors in the summer. Around here they're all too fond of telling you the story of Prince Llewelyn's brave dog, Gelert, and pointing to the grave

ABERGLASLYN

which gave the village its name. Don't be misled; a past landlord of the Royal Goat devised the plausible story to boost his trade. We're going to head for the great gorge of Aberglaslyn!

The Gorge

The way back to Aberglaslyn used to be by way of the old Welsh Highland Railway trackbed, but since this has been reopened the only route is now a rough track by the raging river. The hard bit with handholds comes early on. If you can manage that you can enjoy the excitement of a walk through the gorge and through the attractive woodland that shades its banks. If you want to see that postcard view though, you'll have to make a short detour to the roadside at Pont Aberglaslyn. It's stunning if you haven't seen it before.

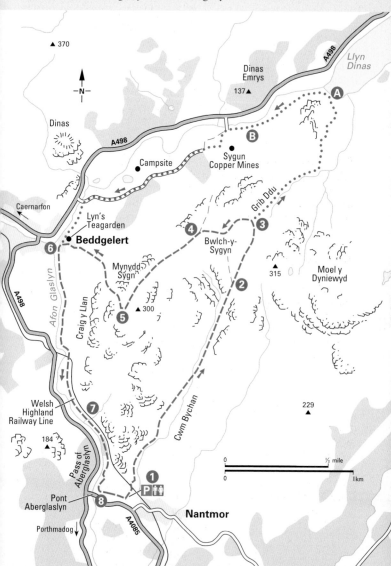

WALK 33 DIRECTIONS

1 The path starts to the left of the toilet block and goes under the old railway bridge, before climbing through Cwm Bychan. After a steady climb the path reaches the iron pylons of the aerial cableway.

2 Beyond the pylons, keep straight on, ignoring paths forking left. A grassy corridor leads to a col, where there's a stile in a fence that is not shown on current maps. Bear left beyond the stile and head for a three-way footpath signpost by the rocks of Grib Ddu.

3 Follow the path on the left signed 'To Beddgelert and Sygun' and go over another ladder stile. Turn left, then follow the path down round a rocky knoll and then down the hillside to a signpost. Just beyond the sign is the cairn at Bwlch-y-Sygun and over to the left is a shallow, peaty pool in a green hollow.

4 The path now heads southwest along the mountain's north-western ridge, overlooking Beddgelert. Ignore any lesser paths along the way.

5 Watch out for a large cairn, highlighting the turn-off right for Beddgelert. The clear stony path weaves through rhododendron and rock, goes through a kissing gate in a wall half-way down, then descends further to the edge of Beddgelert, where a little lane

passing the cottage of Penlan leads to the Afon Glaslyn.

6 Turn left to follow the river for a short way. Don't cross the footbridge over the river but turn left to follow the Glaslyn's east bank. Cross the restored railway line and then continue between it and the river.

7 Below the first tunnel, the path is pushed right to the water's edge. Handholds screwed into the rocks assist passage on a difficult but short section. The path continues through riverside woodland and over boulders until it comes to Pont Aberglaslyn.

8 Here, turn left up some steps and follow a dirt path through the woods. Just before the railway, follow a signed path down and right to the car park.

Onward to Llyn Dinas

Amble back to Beddgelert and take in one of Wales' prettiest lakes.
See map and information panel for Walk 33

DISTANCE *6 miles (9.7km)* MINIMUM TIME *3hrs 30min*
ASCENT/GRADIENT *820ft (250m)* ▲▲▲ LEVEL OF DIFFICULTY +++

WALK 34 DIRECTIONS
(Walk 33 option)

Although this walk is longer than Walk 33 it involves slightly less ascent, mainly because it doesn't lose height on the steep slopes to Bwlch-y-Sygyn. The departure from that route begins by the signpost described in Point ❸. From here, follow the stony path, signed 'To Dinas', which descends gradually north-east down the hillside. Your eyes will be captured by the craggy hills to the right. The serrated top is that of Moel Meirch and those vertical cliffs to the right of it belong to Craig Llyn-llagi. Snowdon's summit comes in and out of view on the left, but its satellite, Y Lliwedd is ever present.

As the path veers left to round a rocky knoll, the reason for this extension becomes clear. Llyn Dinas comes into view, shyly at first, but as the path winds down a heathery hollow, it's finally displayed in all its magnificence, surrounded by oak woods, rhododendrons, and the crags of Snowdon's foothills.

On reaching the shoreline, Point ❹, turn left, go through a kissing gate and then follow a level path alongside the Afon Glaslyn. Ignore the bridges which entice you to the far banks.

Adjacent to the second bridge you'll see the remains of an old crushing plant, including waterwheels. This was part of the Sygun copper mining complex, Point ❹, the main part of which stands on the hillside just above. Small-scale mining had gone on for centuries but the Sygun mines were opened up on a larger scale in 1836. However, they only achieved spasmodic success and production stopped in 1903. They're now open as an award-winning tourist attraction.

The path joins a tarmac track that curves left towards the mines before veering right to resume its course down the valley.

Dinas Emrys, a dominant rocky hill on the far banks of the Glaslyn, once had great ramparts built into the rock. Some believe it is Norman in origin, others date it back further to Arthurian times.

The track becomes a lane and passes a campsite. Leave it where it crosses the river and go over a stile to a path leading into Beddgelert. Don't cross the first bridge in the village but continue downriver to a metal footbridge to rejoin Walk 33, Point ❻.

Gold in the King's Forest

Deep in Coed y Brenin you'll find two waterfalls and maybe a glint of gold.

DISTANCE 4 miles (6.4km)   MINIMUM TIME 2hrs
ASCENT/GRADIENT 656ft (200m) ▲▲▲   LEVEL OF DIFFICULTY +++
PATHS Forest tracks and paths, 2 stiles
LANDSCAPE Forest
SUGGESTED MAP OS Explorer OL18 Harlech, Porthmadog & Bala
START / FINISH Grid reference: SH 735263
DOG FRIENDLINESS Dogs are okay in forest
PARKING Tyddyn Gwladys forest car park near Ganllwyd
PUBLIC TOILETS None en route

WALK 35 DIRECTIONS

If ever there's a case for walking in the rain this is it. There are trees for shelter, two bounding rivers and two waterfalls which look their best when in spate.

The two rivers are the Mawddach, a great river that flows out to sea at Barmouth, and its tributary, the Gain. The trees are those of Coed-y-Brenin – the King's Forest.

Gold has been mined throughout Wales for centuries and there were large finds of good quality gold in the mid-19th century, when Dolgellau became another Klondyke. The rush was on. Morgan Pritchard owned the mining rights to the Mawddach and Cain areas and he started the gold mines at Gwyn-fynydd. Though hopes were high, the mine didn't really produce profitable lodes and work all but stopped in 1914, with only sporadic re-openings to produce rings for royal weddings. Today you'll see the odd prospector panning for gold in the river.

Turn right out of the car park. The tarmac becomes a flinted forestry track, with the Afon Mawddach below on your right.

The trees nearest the river are sessile oak, ash, birch and alder, planted by the Vaughans in the 19th century, when this was part of their Nannau Estate. It's a haven for wildlife. You'll have a chance of seeing the red squirrel, which has been forced out of so many areas by its larger grey cousin. There's also a chance you'll see a heron come to fish. Another angler, though it is harder to spot, is the otter. Brown trout and minnows abound, and each year salmon and sea trout swim through the rapids upriver to spawn.

WHAT TO LOOK OUT FOR

You'll probably see lots of mountain bikes during this walk and you'll certainly cross several bike trails. Coed-y-Brenin pioneered the development of such purpose-built trails and remains one of Britain's top mountain bike centres.

The track passes beneath the Mostyn cottages, originally built for workers from the mines. Just beyond them you'll come to the Ferndale complex, now holiday cottages, but once the workshops and blasting plant. Take the track on the left just above these.

The track swings right to cross the Afon Gain, close to its confluence with the Mawddach. On the other side, detour left along the rough path that takes a closer look at the waterfalls, known as Pistyll Cain. The impressive cascades splash 148ft (45m) against dark rocks into a black pool below; all this in the shadow of thick woodland and, in late spring, embellished by the blooms of rhododendrons.

Return to the main track, where you turn left to the old mine's mill buildings. Years ago this would have been a hive of activity, but it's a rather sad scene now, with graffiti, keep out signs and pipes going nowhere.

At the end of the mill area you come to the second waterfalls, those of Rhaeadr Mawddach. Though they're not as gracefully shaped, high, nor in such pleasant surroundings as Pistyll y Cain, they're nevertheless torrential and impressive. A little further on a restored bridge spans the river. Don't cross it, but double-back left on a path climbing by a plantation. Note the bike route on the right at the start of this path.

Watch out for a recrossing of the bike route, just below a footpath junction, where you turn right on a track marked with a white-topped post (No 30). This comes out of the forest at a small gate, and continues as an enclosed path through high pastures in an area that was once the main Gwyn-fynydd Mine. The track becomes a lane as it passes above the farmhouse of Ty Mawr.

You're high on the hillside now and there's a view over the treetops and across the meandering Mawddach to two shapely mountains, Rhobell Fawr and Dduallt.

Turn right on meeting a quiet lane and follow it almost to Bedd-y-coedwr Farm. A footpath signpost points the way downhill on a faint path above a stream. The path angles right passing through bracken and birch and becoming rough and overgrown in places as it descends to an old mine level just above the Mawddach.

Follow the mine track past decaying buildings to reach the outward route by Rhaeadr Mawddach. Retrace your footsteps to the car park.

Overleaf: Roman Steps (Walk 36)

With the Drovers Over the Roman Steps

Cwm Bychan is one of the treasures of Snowdonia and the Roman Steps one of its oldest highways.

DISTANCE 7 miles (11.3km)   MINIMUM TIME 5hrs

ASCENT/GRADIENT 1,575ft (480m) ▲▲▲   LEVEL OF DIFFICULTY +++

PATHS Rocky paths, tracks and boggy moorland, 9 stiles

LANDSCAPE Gnarled gritstone peaks with heather slopes

SUGGESTED MAP OS Explorer OL18 Harlech, Porthmadog & Bala

START / FINISH Grid reference: SH 646314

DOG FRIENDLINESS Can be off lead in upper heather-clad regions of walk

PARKING Llyn Cwm Bychan

PUBLIC TOILETS Portaloo at car par

NOTE The moorlands around the eastern end of the walk can be very wet and dangerous, with streams under the bogland. The walk is best tackled after a long dry spell

The road from Llanbedr into Cwm Bychan is a joy in itself, passing through oak woods, by the banks of a babbling stream and beneath the small rocky castles of the Rhinog foothills. Llyn Cwm Bychan is stunning. If you see it on an August day, when the colourful heather contrasts with the vivid green of the sessile oaks, and the clouds' shadows play on the rocks of Carreg-y-saeth, then you've seen most of what is good about the Rhinogs. You've also seen it without the hardship of trudging through the knee-deep heather of the Rhinogs' rugged interior. At the risk of contradicting myself, trudging through the Rhinogs has made many a day on these hills exhilarating for me, but it's not for everybody. On this route we will stick to the paths.

Up Those Steps

It seems a shame to lose the paradise that is Cwm Bychan, but we lose it for the shade of its oak woods. As the path climbs towards the Rhinog crags its surface becomes one of great rock slabs that form steps. These Roman Steps are in fact part of a medieval packhorse track, though the Romans, who had a fort in the Trawsfynydd area, might well have used their predecessors. Drovers would have passed this way too, on their way from Harlech to the markets in England, picking up local herds of Welsh Black cattle on the way.

The climb into the pass of Bwlch Tyddiad takes you into country that resembles the canyons of Utah or Arizona. Bwlch Tyddiad narrows and the walls of the surrounding hills close in. Suddenly you're at the top of the pass and looking across a huge rushy hollow surrounded by a million spruce trees, part of the Coed-y-Brenin forest. The trees provide cover for the next couple of miles as the route heads northwards along the east side of the ridge.

From Moel y Gwartheg at the northern edge of the forest there's a good view of the knobbly northern Rhinog ridge and the huge Trawsfynydd reservoir. The Magnox nuclear power station on the far side is being decommissioned now, but the lake used to emit steam into the air as it was used by the station

ROMAN STEPS

for cooling purposes. Controversy still rages, for they're considering turning the site into a nuclear waste plant. A slow and painstaking operation will restore the site to a greenfield status. It is hoped to be completed by 2098!

Paradise Regained

The last stretch of the walk climbs back over another wild heathery pass tucked beneath the craggy mountains of Clip and Craig Wion. From here the path, a narrow ribbon of peat, winds its way through the heather to make a return to the greenery of Cwm Bychan, where paradise is regained.

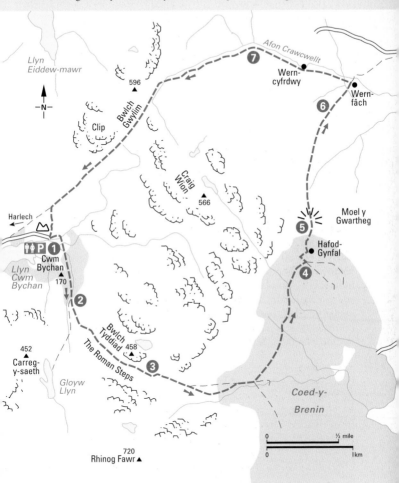

WALK 36 DIRECTIONS

❶ Go through the gate at the back of the car park at Llyn Cwm Bychan and over the paved causeway across the stream. Beyond a stile the path climbs up through squat woodland.

❷ Over another stile you leave woodland behind and cross a stream on a small bridge. The path, always clear, climbs steadily to a gate. Now slabbed with 'the steps', it climbs through a heather-clad rocky ravine and on to the cairn marking the highest point along the rocky pass of Bwlch Tyddiad.

3 From the col, the path descends into a grassy moorland basin beneath Rhinog Fawr, then, beyond a stile, enters the conifers of the Coed-y-Brenin plantation. A well-defined footpath tucks away under the trees and eventually comes to a wide flinted forestry road, along which you turn left.

4 After about a mile (1.6 km), the road swings away to head east; watch out for a way-marked path on the left just beyond the turn. Waymarks guide the route left, then right, to pass the ruins of Hafod-Gynfal. Beyond this you head north to go over a ladder stile and out of the forest.

5 Go straight ahead from the stile, heading north across the grassy moor of Moel y Gwartheg. The ground gets wet as you descend, but it's wetter still further right. You're heading for the isolated cottage of Wern-fach, which stands a little to the left of a small patch of conifers, but for now aim towards the green fields of Cefn Clawdd.

6 You meet a fence, which guides you down to Wern-fâch. Cross a stile, then just above the cottage turn left and go over two ladder stiles. Follow the main stream (Afon Crawcwellt) to Wern-cyfrdwy (house), pass

behind it, then join the walls and fences that shadow the stream. These give the least wet line across the sodden moorland.

7 The going firms up as the ground steepens, climbing to the lonely col of Bwlch Gwylim, a narrow pass between Clip and Craig Wion. Descending the far side, Cwm Bychan and the start of the walk come back into view. The footpath now descends to the south-west, through heather and bracken. After a ladder stile, look for a small waymark where you turn left down steep slopes back to the car park.

High Lakes and Highwaymen

Discover wild Nantcol, the Rhinogs' second valley and see its most splendid lake shoehorned between two rocky peaks.

> **DISTANCE** 5.5 miles (8.8km) **MINIMUM TIME** 3hrs 30min
>
> **ASCENT/GRADIENT** 1,378ft (420m) ▲▲▲ **LEVEL OF DIFFICULTY** +++
>
> **PATHS** Peaty paths through heather and farm tracks, 1 stile
>
> **LANDSCAPE** Gnarled gritstone peaks with heather slopes
>
> **SUGGESTED MAP** OS Explorer OL18 Harlech, Porthmadog & Bala
>
> **START / FINISH** Grid reference: SH 633259
>
> **DOG FRIENDLINESS** Can be off lead in upper heather-clad regions of walk
>
> **PARKING** Small fee for parking at Cil-cychwyn farm or Maes-y-garnedd
>
> **PUBLIC TOILETS** None en route

There are few people living in Nantcol these days – just a handful of farmers. When you set out along the narrow tarmac lane to the mountains you're struck by the sheer isolation of the place. Yet Maes-y-garnedd, the first farm along the route, had an important roll in the Civil War. It was then home of Colonel John Jones who was the Member of Parliament for Merionnydd. The Barmouth and Harlech areas were strong supporters of the Crown, Harlech being one of the last strongholds to surrender to the Parliamentarians. But Jones wasn't one of the Royalists. He married Cromwell's sister and took an active part in the war, and was one of the signatories of Charles I's death warrant. Colonel Jones would gain much power from his associations. Unfortunately the death of Cromwell and the Restoration was untimely, for Charles II remembered him and condemned him to death. Diarist, Samuel Pepys noted that the steaming remains of Jones hung, drawn and quartered body were dragged all over the streets of London.

A Fearsome Place

The road ends just beyond the farm and a good stony path climbs into Bwlch Drws-Ardudwy, a dark pass between the cold grey ramparts of Rhinogs Fawr and Fach. This was a drovers' route along which the Welsh Black cattle would have been driven to the markets of the Marches and the Midlands. The drovers would have been armed and mob-handed, but for the solo traveller in times gone by this would have been a fearsome place: a place frequented by robbers and highwaymen. No traveller would be here without either a fast horse or a gun.

Star of the Show

In the depths of the pass our route turns away from Ardudwy and climbs right up a narrow path, beneath the smaller Rhinog's boulder slopes. The shallow lake, Llyn Cwmhosan is attractive with its pale yellow ring of marsh grass contrasting with the dusky heather. The view back from here to the striated cliffs of the big Rhinog is stunning. However, the star of the show lies in wait, on a high hollow, uphill and around the corner. And like those highwaymen, Llyn Hywel captures your attention. This is one of the great places of Wales. Rhinog Fach appears as a pyramid of boulders and scree, capped by crag. On the other side of the hollow lies Y Llethr, highest of the Rhinogs, displaying a little more greenery, but nonetheless still cutting quite a dash. In between the peaks are gigantic slabs of rock plunging at 45 degrees into the deep waters of the lake.

On the footpath back down we visit another lake, Llyn Perfeddau, basking in yet more heather, that turns out to be even thicker. If you take a wrong choice of route here, you will be up to your knees in it. Sure enough, a little peat path descends to Perfeddau's shores. Look back to see Rhinog Fach reflected perfectly in its waters before making a return to the green fields of Nantcol.

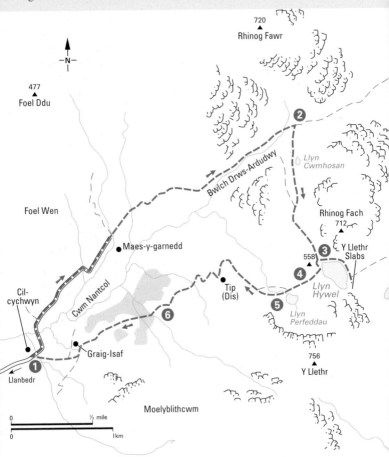

WALK 37 DIRECTIONS

1 From the farm at Cil-cychwyn, follow the narrow lane up the valley until you reach its end. Here continue on a narrow wall-side path, initially hidden, through upper Nantcol. The path traverses the lower south flanks of Rhinog Fawr before entering the dark pass of Bwlch Drws-Ardudwy.

NANTCOL

2 On reaching a marshy basin beneath Rhinog Fawr and Rhinog Fach look for ladder stiles over the wall on the right. The first leads to a very steep short-cut that bypasses Llyn Cwmhosan. Preferably, take the second stile to a narrow path climbing through heather and passing the west shores of Llyn Cwmhosan, and beneath the boulder and screes of Rhinog Fach's west face. Beyond this, the route comes to the shores of Llyn Hywel.

WHILE YOU'RE THERE

Mochras (Shell Island) is a coastal promontory west of Llanbedr and noted, as the English name suggests, for its unusual range of sea-shells, as well as an abundance of wild flowers. Vehicular access is by a tidal causeway.

3 For the best views take the path left of the farm, crossing bouldery screes, and up to the top of the huge Y Llethr Slabs, that plummet into the lake. You could do a complete circuit of Llyn Hywel, but this would mean climbing much higher up the slopes of Y Llethr. It is much easier to retrace your steps to the lake's outlet point, then continue along the west shore.

4 Turn right to follow a sketchy narrow path down to Llyn Perfeddau which is soon visible. Nearing the lake, keep straight ahead on a faint path where the clearer path goes right.

5 Follow the wall running behind the lake then, after about 0.5 mile (800m), go though a gap in the wall to follow a grassy path that rounds a rocky knoll high above Nantcol before passing an old mine. Descend leftward to a prominent track that winds past some mine workings before adopting a straighter course, passing a ruined farm.

6 Through woodland and high pasture, the track passes Graig-Isaf farm before reaching the valley road at Cil-cychwyn.

WHERE TO EAT AND DRINK

The Victoria Hotel is a fine old world inn, whose exterior in summer is made colourful by the profuse blooms of roses, which creep up to the top of the dressed Welsh stone walls. Set at the heart of Llanbedr and popular with locals and tourists, the inn serves traditional bar meals. Children are welcome and dogs by arrangement.

WHAT TO LOOK OUT FOR

The Rhinogs, or Harlech Dome as they are known to geologists, have an overlying strata of rock formed in the Cambrian era over 500 million years ago, long before the surrounding mountain ranges. Mainly consisting of greywackes (grits) these were formed beneath the sea but were uplifted during a collision of continental plates. Look at the layers of angular slabs of rock that form Rhinog Fawr's southern face to see the immense folding in this anticlinal system.

The Sublime Mawddach

Walk in the footsteps of Wordsworth, Darwin and Ruskin who visited here to work and to explore.

DISTANCE *6 miles (9.7km)*   MINIMUM TIME *4hrs*

ASCENT/GRADIENT *656ft (200m)* ▲▲▲   LEVEL OF DIFFICULTY ✦✦✦

PATHS *A bridge, good tracks and woodland paths, 6 stiles*

LANDSCAPE *Estuary and wooded hills*

SUGGESTED MAP *OS Explorer OL23 Cadair Idris & Llyn Tegid*

START / FINISH *Grid reference: SH 613155*

DOG FRIENDLINESS *Dogs should be on lead at all times*

PARKING *Car park on seafront*

PUBLIC TOILETS *At Barmouth's car park, or near Morfa Mawddach Station*

Barmouth (once better known in Welsh as Y Bermo), used to be a seaport, trading the coarse woollen goods of Merionydd with the Americas. In those days the village cottages were strung out across terraces in the cliffs and there was one pub, the Corsygedol Arms, for the traveller. There wasn't enough room to squeeze the main road from Harlech between those rocks and the sea, so it bypassed the village and instead went inland, over the Rhinog mountain passes.

Barmouth: the New Era

In the mid-19th century it all changed. Barmouth built a main street on the beach. Visitors became more frequent and the resort's sea and sand attracted the gentry from the Midlands. Barmouth also came to the notice of the famous: the poet, Wordsworth said of the Mawddach Estuary that it was sublime and equal to any in Scotland. Artists like J M W Turner and Richard Wilson came to capture the changing light and renowned beauty of estuary and mountainside.

In 1867 the railway came, and a new bridge was engineered across the estuary sands. It was half a mile (800m) long and had a swing section across the Mawddach's main channel to allow shipping to pass. Today you can see that Barmouth is not as smart as it was in its heyday. It's still in the most wonderful situation though and, as you step on to the wooden boards of that half-mile foot and railway bridge, you can feel exactly what Wordsworth felt.

Mighty Cadair Idris

The view is best when the sun's shining and the tide's half out. That way the waters of the Mawddach will be meandering like a pale blue serpent amid pristine golden sandbars. Across the estuary your eyes cannot help but be drawn to mighty Cadair Idris. This is not one mountain, but a long ridge with several peaks, each displaying fierce cliffs that soar above the wooded foothills. The biggest is Penygadair at 2,927ft (893m), but the most prominent is Tyrrau Mawr, a shapely peak with a seemingly overhanging crag. As you get to the other side you can look back to Barmouth, and you will see how this town has been built into the rocks of the lower Rhinogs. Across the bridge you're ready to explore those wooded foothills. Through Arthog the path climbs between oak trees and you find yourself looking

across to some waterfalls, thundering into a wooded chasm. At the top you are presented with an elevated view of all that you have seen so far, the estuary, the sandbars, the mountains and the yawning bridge. By the time you return to Barmouth you will have experienced that 'sublime' Mawddach.

WALK 38 DIRECTIONS

1 Follow the promenade round the harbour, then go over the footbridge across the estuary (toll). On reaching the path along the south shore of the estuary, turn left to follow the grassy embankment that leads to a track rounding the wooded knoll of Fegla Fawr on its seaward side.

WHERE TO EAT AND DRINK

Barmouth has many pubs, cafés and fish and chip shops to feed the hungry. Or you could try the George III, which lies on the south side of Penmaenpool toll bridge for a splendid meal.

2 Reaching the terraced houses of Mawddach Crescent, follow the track that passes to their rear. Rejoin the track along the shoreline until you reach a gate on the right marking the start of a bridleway heading inland across the marshes of Arthog.

3 Turn left along the old railway track, then leave it just before the crossing of the little Arthog Estuary and turn right along a tarmac lane by a small car park. Bear left over a ladder stile and follow a raised embankment to a wall which now leads the path to the main Dolgellau road next to St Catherine's Church.

4 Opposite the church gate is a footpath beginning with some steps into woodland. A good waymarked path now climbs by the Arthog.

5 Beyond a stile at the top of the woods, turn right to come to a lane. Turn right along the descending lane, then left along a stony track passing the cottage of Merddyn. The track gets narrower and steeper as it descends into

WHILE YOU'RE THERE

There's a narrow-gauge steam railway linking Fairbourne with Penrhyn Point, reached by ferry from Barmouth. The railway dates back to 1895 when Arthur McDougall, of McDougalls flour fame, built it for horse-drawn trams used to transport materials for Fairbourne village.

more woodland, beneath the boulders of an old quarry and down to the Dolgellau road by Arthog Village Hall.

6 Turn right along the road, then left along a path back to the railway track and the Mawddach Trail. Turn left along the trail and follow it past Morfa Mawddach Station and back across Barmouth's bridge.

WHAT TO LOOK OUT FOR

Near the place you cross the Arthog river (on Walk 39), at the top of the woods, is Llys Bradwen. These days its no more than banks covered by grass, but here are the remains of large wooden hall from a Dark Ages house. In those times it would have been occupied by the local chieftain, Ednowain ap Bradwen.

Onward to Cregennen

*High above the estuary and in the shadow of Cadair Idris
lie two fine lakes.*

See map and information panel for Walk 38

DISTANCE 9 miles (14.5km)	**MINIMUM TIME** 5hrs 30min
ASCENT/GRADIENT 1,116ft (340m) ▲▲▲	**LEVEL OF DIFFICULTY** ✦✦✦

WALK 39 DIRECTIONS
(Walk 38 option)

'Old Cader is a grand fellow and shows himself superbly with everchanging light. Do come and see him.' So wrote Charles Darwin. Although we're not going to the summit, that's just what we're going to do with this extra loop.

From the ladder stile at the top of the woods, Point **❺**, turn left and go over the slabbed bridge. From here follow a grass path, then turn left on a track. Where this veers right to climb across fields, keep straight ahead following the wall on your left past ruins.

Frequent waymarkers are placed on this high, field path, but your attention will be occupied by the view across the Mawddach. Turning your attention back on to this side of the estuary, the imposing rock mountain that the path is heading for is known as Bryn Brith. Although you cannot see them now, the lakes of Cregennen are nestled at its foot.

Briefly follow a walled track on the left, then go right across a field to a ladder stile. Frequent waymarks lead to another high ladder stile from which the path drops down to the winding Cregennen Road, Point **❹**.

Turn right along the road, which climbs steeply between the rocks and rough pastures, to reach the Cregennen Lakes, Point **❸**.

You cannot but be impressed as you view the lakes from above on one of the huge roadside boulders. The shoreline marshes are covered with many interesting plants, including marsh cinquefoil, water lobelia and marsh St John's wort. There's an island on the nearest lake with several tall but windswept Scots pines. Behind the lakes your eyes will be rivetted to Tyrrau Mawr, whose flowing scree slopes are fringed with ragged cliffs. The main Cadair peak of Penygadair just peeps out from behind the towering climbers' crags of Cyfrwy. There's an old myth that if you spend the night on Cadair Idris you will return a madman or a poet. The author has and we'll leave it to you to decide which, if either, he has become.

Past the lakes turn right at a road junction then right again and descend a steep lane to rejoin Walk 38 just beyond Point **❺**.

The Lost Village of Vyrnwy

A short walk by one of Wales' largest lakes, revealing ghosts from the past.

DISTANCE 3 miles (4.8km)	**MINIMUM TIME** 2hrs
ASCENT/GRADIENT 460ft (140m) ▲▲▲	**LEVEL OF DIFFICULTY** +++

PATHS Country lane, forest tracks and field path

LANDSCAPE Afforested hills

SUGGESTED MAP OS Explorer 239 Lake Vyrnwy & Llanfyllin

START / FINISH Grid reference: SJ 017189

DOG FRIENDLINESS Farmland: dogs should be on lead

PARKING Car park in valley bottom beneath Llanwddyn Visitor Centre

PUBLIC TOILETS By visitor centre

WALK 40 DIRECTIONS

When 18th-century traveller Thomas Pennant came to the Efyrnwy (Vyrnwy) there was no reservoir. Here was a wild Welsh cwm situated 'in hilly naked country', property of the powerful Vaughans. Llanwddyn village snuggled in a hollow where the Afon Cedig met the Efyrnwy.

In 1860 Llanwddyn was still a picturesque place, now with ten farms, 37 houses, three inns, two chapels and a small parish church. The hills were free of conifers and a little two-arched, humpback bridge spanned the Efyrnwy. Further up the valley was Eunant Hall, a grand mansion owned by Sir Edmund Buckley – life was all very peaceful and orderly. But behind the scenes, Liverpool, the second city of the British Empire, was searching for water to feed its factories. Their engineers turned to the Efyrnwy. Royal Assent followed and by 1880 work had started. Llanwddyn was invaded by engineers and 1,000 navvies, who were to build a huge dam and a 68-mile (109km) gravity-fed tunnel leading all the way back to their city. Over 510,000 tons of rock were quarried from the local mountains to build the then largest masonry dam in the world.

WHERE TO EAT AND DRINK

The café by the tourist information centre serves various meals, hot and cold beverages and snacks. For a big meal from local produce go to the Lake Vyrnwy Hotel.

As the walls went up, enclosing this little world from the outside, life for those in Llanwddyn went on, but the village had to go – it was to be flooded under the gigantic new reservoir. So the engineers built a new village, including a church, to the south of the dam. The reservoir structures were completed in 1888. They are a masterpiece of Victorian Gothic design, but as the valves were closed and the waters rose, lapping slowly over the foundations of the demolished dwellings, a village was lost.

And so in the 21st century visitors flock to see the new Llanwddyn, its visitor centres, its café and that dam. Severn Trent Water owns the place now and manages the land in co-operation with the RSPB. Nature trails are being developed within the vast conifer forests that surround the lake. This route will mostly follow the Craig Garth-Bwlch Nature Trail, highlighted by dark blue waymarkers.

WHAT TO LOOK OUT FOR

From the bird hide near the main car park you could well see siskins. They are one of our smallest finches and they're seen around here between February and August. The adults have dark greenish uppers, often streaked with black. Their breasts are yellow, streaked with brown, and their bellies are white.

WHILE YOU'RE THERE

Go and see Andy Hancock's sculptures on the very short Sculpture Trail, which involves touring by car to various sights around the lake. They are not the usual totem poles paid for by lottery grants and EU money, but fine works of art.

Follow the tarmac lane past the information centre, beyond which you'll see the first of the waymarkers. The lane climbs through oak woods, where you might see the crimson flashes of the redstart darting through the boughs. Ignore the turn off to the left down to Coed Grwn-oer, but continue with the lane, which swings right, over the shoulder of Craig Garth-bwlch (hill). Down below you the Afon Efyrnwy meanders between small, afforested hills and green, farm fields. The tarmac ends at the Ty-newydd Farm turn off. Here the route continues on a stony forest track which skirts the hill before entering the forest itself.

A new valley appears ahead as the track descends to round the corner to Craig Garth-bwlch's east side. It is that of the Cownwy, a tributary of the Efyrnwy, and it's equally green and pretty. The track descends further to meet another track. Follow it to the right.

Take the right fork just before Bryn Cownwy Farm and climb through the conifers. At a junction, keep ahead, still following blue waymarkers. The track later swings sharply left, eventually arriving at another meeting of paths. The ongoing route is to the right, but first wander left for a splendid view over a gate into the valley.

Gently descending through the trees, bear left at a junction. Lower down the track swings right to fall at the edge of the forest, shortly after it returns you to the village.

Before you go home be sure to visit the dam and follow a short waymarked path through oak woods to the Lake Vyrnwy Hotel. From here you get the classic view of the lake. When I saw the sleepy waters from here I was reminded of the local legend that circulated during the building of the dam. It had always been believed that the spirit of a ghost known as Yspryd Cynon lay beneath a prominent boulder in the valley. When the itinerant labourers blasted the stone in order to remove it from the site they reported that a large toad was seen sitting in a nearby pool rubbing its eyes. Locals were convinced that the toad was Yspryd Cynon.

Overleaf: Precipice Walk (Walk 41)

A Stroll Around the Precipice

One of the finest short walks in Wales, the Precipice Walk follows a balcony route with spectacular views of valley, mountain and estuary.

DISTANCE *3 miles (4.8km)*   MINIMUM TIME *2hrs*

ASCENT/GRADIENT *Negligible* ▲▲▲   LEVEL OF DIFFICULTY ✦✦✦

PATHS *Stony tracks and good paths, occasionally rough, 4 stiles*

LANDSCAPE *Mountainside and pasture*

SUGGESTED MAP *OS Explorer OL18 Harlech, Porthmadog & Bala*

START / FINISH *Grid reference: SH 745211*

DOG FRIENDLINESS *Private land – dogs must always be on a lead*

PARKING *Coed y Groes car park on Dolgellau–Llanfachreth road*

PUBLIC TOILETS *At car park*

NOTE *Wear strong footwear as part of route follows narrow path with big drops down to Mawddach Valley. Not a walk for vertigo sufferers*

There's been a house at Nannau since the 12th century, when the estate was owned by descendants of Cadwgan, Prince of Powys. That original building was burned down in 1404 after trouble between the owner, Hywel Sele, the 8th Lord of Nannau and his cousin Owain Glyndwr. The pair had never liked or trusted each other, mainly due to Hywel's allegiance to England's House of Lancaster, but they were brought together by the Abbot of Cymer (the abbey in the valley below).

Owain and Hywel

While out hunting together Glyndwr spotted a doe and pointed it out for Hywel, who was a fine bowman, to kill. Hywel pretended to aim at the animal but then suddenly swung around towards Owain. The arrow was straight and true but, as Glyndwr had been wearing armour under his tunic, it did not pierce his skin. After burning down the house it is said that Glyndwr killed his cousin and disposed of his body in a hollow tree. The skeleton wasn't found for 40 years and the house wasn't rebuilt until 1693.

The Nannau family, who became the Nanneys, still lived on the estate, but had financial problems. Hugh Nanney was heavily fined and imprisoned for trying to resolve his difficulties by felling 10,000 oaks. When the male line died out the female line, which had married into the powerful Vaughan family, took over. The Vaughans replanted many of the trees and, in 1796, built the grand mansion you see today.

Spectacular Views

As you start high there's very little ascent to do and the early part of the walk eases across woodland and farm pastures. As the path rounds Foel Cynwch and past the Sitka spruce of Coed Dôl-y-clochydd, spectacular views of the wooded Mawddach and Wen valleys open up. The high ridge seen on the other side of the Mawddach is Y Garn, one of the Rhinog outliers. It looks gentle enough from here, but Y Garn's other face is of thick heather and precipitous rock.

PRECIPICE WALK

Exciting Terrace

Beyond another ladder stile the path itself gets spectacular, taking the form of an exciting terrace, high above the river. Crag, the odd birch and rowan, and flecks of pink from rhododendron bushes all decorate a magnificent scene, which soon adds the great northern cliffs of the Cadair Idris mountains to its repertoire. The precipice lasts an exquisite mile (1.6km) with little twists and turns to add a little spice to the walk. Before long you can trace the Mawddach past Dolgellau's plains, past the sandbars of its estuary, to the sea beyond.

Old Oak Trees

It seems a shame to leave all this behind, but the little path veers left and descends to the shores of Llyn Cynwch where anglers will be casting for trout. The lake also has an avenue of old oak trees, all that remains of what was quite a large forest until Hugh Nanney took to his axe. When you reach the far shores of the lake stop to take one last look south. Here you will see the cliffs of Cadair Idris reflected and rippling with the lapping waters of the lake.

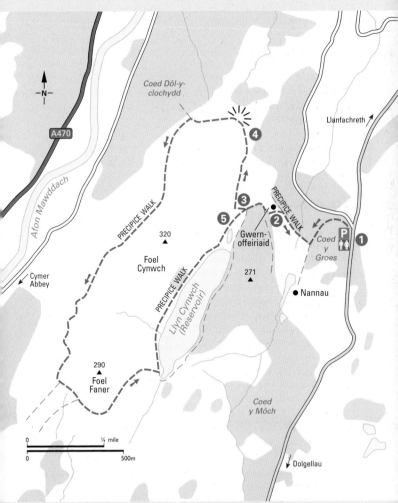

WALK 41 DIRECTIONS

① From the top end of the car park turn right on a level footpath which curves around to join another wide track. The Precipice Walk is a private path around the Nannau Estate, but its use has been authorised by the estate owners since 1890, on the basis that all walkers observe the country code. It's probably one of the finest short routes in Wales and, as such, has been one of Dolgellau's most famous attractions since those early days when Victorian tourists came for their constitutional perambulations. The track swings right at the edge of some fields.

② Where the track comes to an estate cottage, Gwern-offeiriaid, turn left off it. Follow a clear path leading to the hillside north of Llyn Cynwch. There you see the grand mansion of Nannau, built for the Vaughans in 1796.

③ At a footpath signpost fork right. The path climbs the hillside and turns northwards by the side of a dry-stone wall.

④ Beyond a stile the footpath curves around a crag-studded hill, with open slopes that give fine views across a green valley below to the village of Llanfachreth and the rugged mountainsides of Rhobell Fawr and Dduallt that lie behind. The footpath edges rounds Foel Cynwch and passes the Sitka spruce woodlands of Coed Dôl-y-clochydd. Ignore a path signed to Glasdir and keep left,

reaching the dramatic, but even ledge path traversing the high hill slopes above the Mawddach Valley. Where the slopes finally ease, there's a promontory on the right, with a bench placed to enjoy the view. The path now arcs round to the southern side of Foel Faner, drops to the lake and turns sharp left to follow the western shore.

⑤ The path meets the outward route by the hill footpath sign. Retrace the outward route past the estate cottage of Gwern-offeiriaid and through the woods back to the car park.

A View of Bala's Lake – Llyn Tegid

Climbing above Bala to get the best view of Wales' largest natural lake.

DISTANCE *5 miles (8km)* MINIMUM TIME *3hrs*

ASCENT/GRADIENT *656ft (200m)* ▲▲▲ LEVEL OF DIFFICULTY +++

PATHS *Woodland and field paths, 7 stiles*

LANDSCAPE *Woods and upland pasture*

SUGGESTED MAP *OS Explorer OL23 Cadair Idris & Llyn Tegid, or OS Explorer OL18 Harlech, Porthmadog and Bala*

START / FINISH *Grid reference: SH 929361*

DOG FRIENDLINESS *Dogs should be on lead at all times*

PARKING *Car park at entrance to Bala town from east*

PUBLIC TOILETS *At car park*

'It was a beautiful evening… the wind was blowing from the south, and tiny waves were beating against the shore, which consisted of small brown pebbles. The lake has certainly not its name, which signifies Lake of Beauty, for nothing'

George Borrow, *Wild Wales*, 1862

Borrow had been staying at the White Lion in Bala and had been impressed with the place and its people. Bala is an austere town, close to the banks of two great rivers, the Tryweryn and the Dee, and the shore of Wales' largest natural lake, Llyn Tegid.

Religion and Wool

The town's many chapels give a hint to its religious roots. You'll see the statue of Dr Lewis Edwards, founder of the Methodist College, and, opposite the White Lion, one of the Revd Thomas Charles, a founder of the British and Foreign Bible Society. Bala's employment was based around the woollen industry, and the town was noted for its stockings. Thomas Pennant came here in 1786 and painted a fascinating picture of life in the town: 'Round the place, women and children are in full employ, knitting along the roads; and mixed with them Herculean figures appear, assisting their omphales in this effeminate employ.'

Recreational Activities

Llyn Tegid is every bit as beautiful as Borrow suggests and it's popular for watersports. When the south-westerlies blow, Bala has waves like an angry ocean. It's favoured by anglers too. Pike, perch, trout, salmon and roach are plentiful, but the fish Llyn Tegid is famous for is the Gwyniad, which is not unlike a freshwater herring. It is said these fish were trapped here after the last ice age. You come to the old Norman motte-and-bailey castle of Tomen y Mur soon after turning your back the lake. Some say that the mound goes back to Roman times, but it is known that the castle was captured from the Normans

BALA

by Llewelyn ap Iowerth in 1202. One of those Welsh steam railways has its terminus right next to the old castle site and it's fascinating to see the old steam engines puffing along the lakeside. However, we are in search of higher things, so climb through woods and upland fields until you get your view. From up high you can see Tegid's blue waters, seemingly perfect and still from this distance, and stretching 4.5 miles (7.2km) along its rift valley towards Dolgellau. White farmhouses are dotted on pleasant pastured hills. The Dee, so wide down river from Bala, has anonymous beginnings in the peat bogs beneath Dduallt, whose dark crags rise high on the north-west horizon.

It's time to descend, through more oak woods, and further, beneath western hemlock and larch, finally to reach the lakeshores and the welcome comforts of the town.

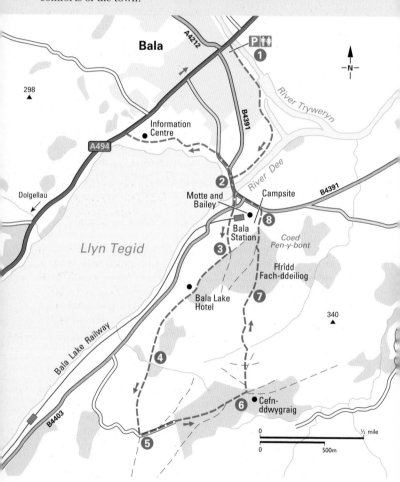

WALK 42 DIRECTIONS

❶ Go to the north corner of the car park in Bala to access the riverside path. Turn right to follow a raised embankment along

the west bank of the Tryweryn. After a dog-leg to the right, passing through two kissing gates, the footpath continues, first by the banks of the Tryweryn, then by the north banks of the Dee.

WHAT TO LOOK OUT FOR

In the woodlands of Ffridd Fach-ddeilog there are many broadleaved trees and conifers. The soil is quite rich here and unlike the upper slopes, where the Sitka spruce dominates, species like Japanese larch and Western hemlock thrive. The larch will be easily recognised in winter as it isn't evergreen and will have dropped its needles on the forest floor. The hemlock, a narrow conical tree with small pendulous cones, grows to about 164ft (50m) in the British Isles.

2 On reaching the road, cross the bridge over the River Dee, then a smaller, older bridge. Go through a kissing gate to cross a small field to Bala Station on Bala Lake Railway. A footbridge allows you to cross the track before traversing two small fields.

WHILE YOU'RE THERE

For great views of the lake and surrounding mountains why not take a trip on the excellent Bala Lake Railway? The narrow-gauge steam train uses the former trackbed of the old Great Western Railway which was built to link Ruabon and Barmouth. Trains depart from Llanuwychllyn and run the full length of the lake back to Bala Station. The service is usually operational between April and the end of September.

3 Turn right along a cart track, and continue to pass behind the Bala Lake Hotel. A waymarker points the direction up a grassy bank on the left, and the path continues to a stile and then follows a fence on the right.

4 Descend slightly to cross a stream beside a small cottage, go up again then along a level fence

to a stile. Bear left up through some bracken and wind up steeply at first, then continue more easily to a tarmac lane.

5 Turn left along the lane to a cattle grid from where you continue on a stony track, passing through felled plantations.

6 Just before the isolated house of Cefn-ddwygraig, turn left off the track to a ladder stile. Follow a grooved grass track across gorse-covered slopes. Keep left at a fork and then drop down to a stile. The well-waymarked path continues north, with Bala town ahead.

WHERE TO EAT AND DRINK

Plas Yn Dre Restaurant in Bala's High Street specialises in local dishes, which you can eat in the restaurant or, if it's nice, on the patio outside. We had a really tasty Welsh lamb, complete with roast potatoes.

7 Go over a partially hidden step stile into the commercial forestry plantations of Coed Pen-y-bont. A narrow footpath descends to the bottom edge of the woods (ignore the forestry track you meet on the way down).

8 At the bottom of the woods turn right along a track that reaches the road by the Pen-y-Bont Campsite. Turn left along the road, cross the Dee again, bear left and then follow the lakeside footpath past the information centre. When you reach the main road, turn right to explore the fascinating town centre.

WALK 43

The Dysynni Valley and Castell y Bere

Explore the valleys where the princes of Wales held out against Edward I and a barefoot girl inspired a world-renowned society.

DISTANCE *5 miles (8km)*	MINIMUM TIME *3hrs*	
ASCENT/GRADIENT *656ft (200m)* ▲▲▲	LEVEL OF DIFFICULTY ✦✦✦	
PATHS *Field paths and tracks, 14 stiles*		
LANDSCAPE *Pastured hills and valleys*		
SUGGESTED MAP *OS Explorer OL23 Cadair Idris & Llyn Tegid*		
START / FINISH *Grid reference: SH 677069*		
DOG FRIENDLINESS *Dogs should be on leads at all times*		
PARKING *Car park by community centre in Abergynolwyn*		
PUBLIC TOILETS *At community centre*		

Abergynolwyn lies in the emerald valley of the Dysynni and beneath the great spruce woods of the Dyfi Forest. It's a village built out of Welsh slate and from the proceeds of that slate. However, on this walk we turn our backs on the purple rock to head northwards for the rolling green hills and the delectable oak woods of Coed Cedris that cloak their lower slopes. At the top of these woods you're transported into a high cwm. The Nant yr Eira trickles out from the rushes, but by the time you're descending into the valley of the Cadair, it's splashing and cascading through its own shady ravine.

Mary Jones

Through more woodland, you come to the valley bottom at Llanfihangel-y-pennant, where there's an attractive stone-built chapel that dates back to the 12th century. These days it's dedicated to Mary Jones, a poor weaver's daughter of the 18th century. As a 15-year-old she decided she wanted a Welsh-language Bible of her own. Though she had no shoes to wear, Mary made her way across hills to Bala, some 30 miles (48km) away, where she had heard that some were available. Unfortunately for Mary, the Revd Thomas Charles had none left to sell but, touched by her persistence, he gave her his own copy. Charles was very impressed by Mary's tenacity and it inspired him to consider the needs of Christians around the world who couldn't read the Bible in their own language. Along with several like-minded evangelicals, in 1804 he founded a group called the British and Foreign Bible Society. As well as Bibles in Welsh, one of the first they produced was in Mohawk. Mary's cottage, Tyn-y-ddol, and a monument to her, can be found a short way north up the road.

Welsh Fortress

The main route heads in the opposite direction. Here the Afon Cadair has formed a wide flat valley. In the middle of the plains, perched on a great crag are the ruins of a true Welsh fortress, Castell y Bere. Built in the early 13th century by Llewelyn the Great, it held out longer than any other when Edward I and his armies invaded Wales. By this time Llewelyn ap Grufydd had become Prince of Wales, but had been killed at Builth, leaving his brother Dafydd to defend the castle. Dafydd fought long and hard but was defeated in 1283. He escaped capture for a while and hid out on the slopes of Cadair Idris. Eventually, he was betrayed by his own people and was dragged to Shrewsbury where he was brutally hung, drawn and quartered. So Wales was defeated and the castle laid waste.

Narrow Defile

The path continues along the now peaceful pastures of this pleasant valley to meet the Dysynni which has wriggled through a narrow defile between two hills. The winding green track that squeezes through with it is perhaps the finest mile in this book; you're almost disappointed to get back to Abergynolwyn so soon.

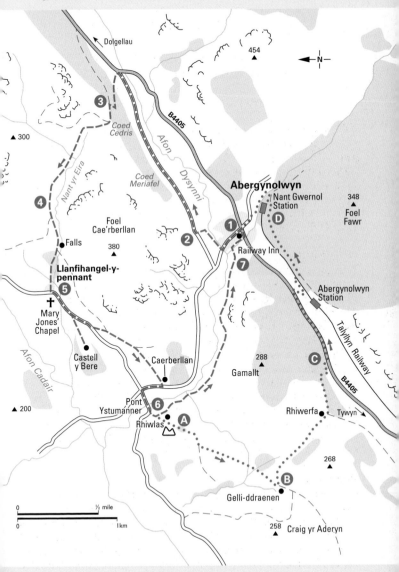

WALK 43

WALK 43 DIRECTIONS

1 Cross the road to the Railway Inn and take the lane signposted to Llanegryn. At the far side of the bridge spanning the Dysynni river, turn right through a kissing gate and trace above the north banks. At a second step stile the path turns left before climbing some steps alongside some tall leylandii to reach a country lane.

2 Turn right along the lane which heads east through the Dysynni Valley and beneath the woodlands of Coed Meriafel. At the junction with the B4405 turn left, over a stile and climb north-west across a field. Continue over two more stiles to a woodland path. Follow this to reach a forestry track near the top of the woods.

3 Turn left along the track which climbs out of the woods before veering right to a gate and adjacent stile, giving entry into a large field. Go straight ahead to pick up a ruined overgrown wall. Where this ends, bear left to descend a high grassy cwm with a stream developing just to your left. Ford another stream which joins from the right near a ruin.

4 The green path develops a flinted surface. Leave it where it starts to climb and rejoin a streamside path on the left. This descends into the woods and stays close to the stream. After passing several cascades it comes out of the woods to reach a track,

which in turn leads to the road at Llanfihangel-y-pennant just opposite the chapel.

5 Turn left past the chapel and Castell y Bere (detour through gates on the right for a closer look). Just beyond the castle, take a path on the left that climbs to the gate at the top right-hand corner of the field. Turn right along a green track which passes Caerberllan farm to come to the road. Turn right, go left at the crossroads and cross Pont Ystumanner (a bridge).

6 On the other side, a footpath signpost highlights a track on the left, which passes below Rhiwlas farm and continues as a green path above the river. The path eases across the slopes of Gamallt and swings left with the valley.

7 Beyond a river gorge, the path approaches the back of Abergynolwyn village and turns left to cross an old iron bridge across the river. Turn right along an unsurfaced street to return to the village centre.

A Bird's Eye View

Stay higher for longer and see Castell y Bere as an invader would have seen it.

See map and information panel for Walk 43

DISTANCE 7 miles (11.3km)   **MINIMUM TIME** 4hrs
ASCENT/GRADIENT 1,247ft (380m) ▲▲▲   **LEVEL OF DIFFICULTY** ✦✦✦

WALK 44 DIRECTIONS
(Walk 43 option)

At Point **6** on the main route go through the gate towards Rhiwlas, but, just before the house, climb a grassy bank to cross a stile on the right. Take a path that climbs steeply over fields with a line of trees to the left, Point **A**. Take a look back now and see Castell y Bere on its huge rock outcrop, commanding the valley.

After going through a small copse and over a stile, the route maintains direction past a stand of gorse then swings right through a grassy channel between two rocky knolls to reach a stile in a fence. Turn left beyond the stile and follow the fence across pastures. At the far end, descend to a streamlet and go through a gate. Bear left to a stile then climb past a waymarking post at the top of the far banks.

Cross another stile then follow a bank and green track towards the cottage of Gelli-ddraenen, Point **B**. The impressive hill looming beyond is Craig yr Aderyn, the Bird Rock. On the high summit crags is the only colony of cormorants that breed inland. Go through a gate just before the cottage and turn left up a track to meet a tarred lane. Now go straight ahead on this and descend past Rhiwerfa farm to the B4405, Point **C**.

Turn left along the road to the entrance to Abergynolwyn Station. Go up the station approach to a signed footpath following the nearside of the railway. In about 400yds (366m) turn right on a forestry track, crossing the railway. At a junction double back left. (Keep following red waymarks.) There are soon some good views over Abergynolwyn village.

Beyond a turning circle, Point **D**, the track becomes a footpath that climbs again before a left fork leads down to Nant Gwernol Station. Just as you reach the station turn sharp right to a footbridge, from where a lovely waymarked footpath descends by the river. Here you'll see some waterfalls before reaching the tarmac lane to the village centre.

Long Mountain Woodlands

A walk through the woods with puzzles and glimpses into the past.

WALK 45

DISTANCE *6.75 miles (10.9km)* MINIMUM TIME *4hrs*

ASCENT/GRADIENT *1,312ft (400m)* ▲▲▲ LEVEL OF DIFFICULTY ✦✦✦

PATHS *Forestry tracks, woodland paths and country lanes, 5 stiles*

LANDSCAPE *Afforested hillside*

SUGGESTED MAP *OS Explorer 216 Welshpool & Montgomery*

START / FINISH *Grid reference: SJ 238023*

DOG FRIENDLINESS *Dogs could run free in forest*

PARKING *Roadside parking in Forden village (B4388)*

PUBLIC TOILETS *None en route*

WALK 45 DIRECTIONS

The 5-mile (8km) Long Mountain ridge looks down on the plains of England and the snaking valley of the Severn. It's not a shapely ridge but does have miles of fascinating woodland footpaths and airy views of the green fields of England and the rolling hills of Wales.

Although the route directions here may sound a little complex, the route-finding is simple, for here the Offa's Dyke National Trail markers will guide you all the way to the Beacon Ring at the top of the mountain. From the Cock Hotel, take the B4388 north through Forden, turning off towards the top end along a lane on the right. This bends left to climb uphill on what is the course of Offa's Dyke.

Offa, an 8th-century Saxon king, was having trouble with the Celtic warlords from Wales, who had for centuries been making forays into the Marches. His solution was a boundary, the Dyke, which would run the length of the border from

Chepstow to the Flintshire coast. The earthworks here are either side of the road in places and will continue through the woodland that you are about to enter.

WHAT TO LOOK OUT FOR

Offa's Dyke runs right through the forest and is often near your path if you look hard enough. It's especially noticeable in Green Wood.

Turn left when you get to the Offa's Dyke footpath sign to follow the right of two tracks. This passes the Lodge and goes into Green Wood, which is part of the expansive Leighton Estate. This place is largely the work of estate owner and Liverpool banker John Naylor who, in the 1850s, built a great Gothic mansion with ornate gardens. These he surrounded with the fine woodland you see today, and included a grove of giant redwoods and monkey puzzles, some of which you'll see en route. Perhaps one the most notable things to come from the Leighton Estate was an accident of nature. It happened here in 1888 when the cones of Nootka cypress were fertilised by pollen from Monterey cypress, two species that would never have co-existed in the wild. What resulted was the *Cupressocyparis leylandii*, a fast-growing scourge of gardens.

The path, still accompanied by the earthworks of Offa's Dyke, stays parallel to the road for a while, but then swings left in Pole Plantation. Beyond this take the signposted right fork. You soon leave this for a small path on the left, which descends through the trees, in steps in the later stages, to reach another forestry track. Turn right along this to pass around the tree-filled hollow and a tall brick retaining wall that are the remains of Offa's Pool, part of an elaborate water system that provided power for the estate's farm machinery.

Fork left over a bridge, but then ignore a descending path and continue to a dark pool. Bear off right on a narrower path beside it which leads out to a lane at the far side of the estate.

Turn left along the lane then climb right, along a tarmac forest road to a junction of tracks. The one on the right you will use on the return route, but on this occasion go through a bridle-gate ahead and climb at the field edge beside Phillip's Gorse. At the top, go left through another

gate, leaving the top corner of the wood over a stile. Follow the ongoing hedge, first on one side and then the other to the afforested knoll of Beacon Ring. The single-banked circular fort, also known as Caer Digoll, belongs to the Iron Age, about 2,500 years ago. A round barrow, built to cover a burial, pre-dates the fort by about a thousand years taking it back to the Bronze Age. Sadly, the plantation trees stop you from imagining how this place would have looked with its ramparts, wooden huts and gateways. It surely would have been a wonderful viewpoint. Today you have to be content with the view to Welshpool and the Severn, where the afternoon sun can render the river as a shiny blue serpent slithering away to the green Welsh border hills. You can encircle the ring's westward flank, but the view north is hidden by the Cwmdingle Plantation

Retrace your footsteps to the previously mentioned junction by Phillips's Gorse. Turn sharp left along the scrub-lined grassy track that leads out to the lane running the length of Long Mountain. Turn right along the lane, a former Roman road, linking their fort Lavobrinta at Forden with one at Wroxeter. Keep ahead at a crossroads, the quiet hedge-lined lane easing back to the car.

Powis Castle and the Montgomery Canal

See how the Earls of Powis lived as you walk through their deer park and past their huge red palace on the hill.

DISTANCE *4 miles (6.4km)* MINIMUM TIME *2hrs*

ASCENT/GRADIENT *328ft (100m)* ▲▲▲ LEVEL OF DIFFICULTY +++

PATHS *Tarmac drive, field path, canal tow path, 3 stiles*

LANDSCAPE *Country town, parkland and canal*

SUGGESTED MAP *OS Explorer 216 Welshpool & Montgomery*

START / FINISH *Grid reference: SJ 226075*

DOG FRIENDLINESS *Dogs not allowed on the Powis Castle Estate*

PARKING *Large pay car park off Church Street, Welshpool*

PUBLIC TOILETS *By information centre in car park*

A prosperous and bustling market town set amid rolling green hills, wood and hedgerows, Welshpool has always been synonymous with the River Severn, which flows through it. It was the Severn that brought trade to the town, for it was navigable by boat. The town was, until 1835, known as Pool and some of the old mileposts still refer to Pool. The 'Welsh' was added to distinguish the place from Poole in Dorset.

A Majestic Setting

When you walk up the busy High Street today you'll notice the fine architecture, most of it dating from Georgian times, like the Royal Oak Hotel, but also many older half-timbered buildings. Almost every tourist who comes to Welshpool comes to see the fine castle of Powis. On this route you turn off through the impressive wrought-iron gates before strolling along the long drive through the estate's parklands. Proud oaks are scattered on the well-mown grasslands and a majestic scene is set when you see deer roaming among the trees, maybe antlered stags, or those cute little fallow deer.

Today the castle is a grand red mansion, with castellated ramparts, tall chimneys, rows of fine leaded windows and 17th-century balustraded terraces looking over manicured lawns and neatly clipped yews. Lead statues of a shepherd and shepherdess survive from those early days and keep watch over the colourful shrubs and perennial borders.

Warring Princes

However, the scene would have been so different in 1200, when the castle was first built for the warring Princes of Powys. The battlements would have been there, but there would have been no elegant windows or pretty gardens, for this place was designed to repel enemies, both English and Welsh: more often than not Powis sided with the English, even against the Glyndwr rebellion. The fact that Powis has been continuously occupied has meant that it has made a successful transition from fortress to a comfortable grand mansion.

In 1587 the powerful Herbert family, who became the Earls of Powis, took possession of the castle. They were to reside here until 1988, when the 6th Earl died, and were responsible for the transition. Only for a brief period, when they were attacked by Cromwellian forces and replaced by their bitter rivals, the Myddeltons of Chirk, were the Royalist Herberts displaced.

On leaving the castle behind, you are in rural Wales and you descend to the tow path of the Montgomery Canal at the Belan Locks. Built by three different companies and opened in stages from 1796, the canal was designed for narrowboats. Today it is a quiet backwater and a pleasant return route to the wharf at Welshpool.

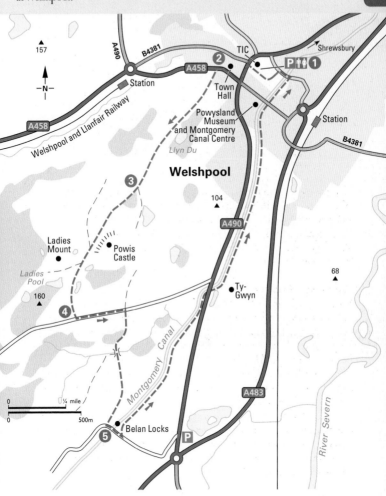

WALK 46 DIRECTIONS

❶ From the main car park go past the tourist information centre then go left along Church Street. At the crossroads in the centre of town turn right to head up Broad Street, which later becomes High Street.

❷ When you get to a point just beyond the town hall, turn left past a small car parking area and pass through the impressive wrought iron gates of the Powis Castle Estate. Now follow the tarmac drive through the park grounds and past Llyn Du (which means the black lake in English).

Overleaf: Powis Castle

3 Take the right fork, the high road, which leads to the north side of the castle. You can detour from the walk here to visit the world-famous gardens and the castle with its fine paintings and furniture and works of Indian art collected by Robert Clive. Continue on the walk on the high road and follow it past two more pools on the left and the Ladies Pool on the right to reach a country lane.

4 Turn left along the country lane. Opposite the next estate entrance leave the lane over a stile beside a gate on the right, from which a grass track winds down to a bridge. Climb away beside the right-hand fence. Continue over another stile in the corner along an old way, which gently falls to a lane beside the Montgomery

Canal. This canal, which runs for 33 miles (53km) from Welsh Frankton in Shropshire to Newtown in Powys, is gradually being restored. You may see a number of narrowboats cruising along this section.

5 Turn over the bridge at Belan Locks, immediately dropping left to the canal tow path. Head north along the canal, later passing beneath the main road. Entering Welshpool, remain on the tow path, passing the Powysland Museum and Montgomery Canal Centre (on the opposite bank), with its exhibits of local agriculture, crafts and the canal and railway systems. Beyond a short aqueduct and former railway bridge, climb out to the road and turn left back to the car park.

Montgomery – Land of the Marcher Lords

See Iron Age and medieval castles and look down on a wide landscape from Montgomery's Town Hill.

DISTANCE	*5.25 miles (8.4km)* **MINIMUM TIME** *3hrs*
ASCENT/GRADIENT	*951ft (290m)* ▲▲▲ **LEVEL OF DIFFICULTY** +++
PATHS	*Well-defined paths, farm tracks and country lanes, 1 stile*
LANDSCAPE	*Pastoral hills overlooking wide plains of the Severn*
SUGGESTED MAP	*OS Explorer 216 Welshpool & Montgomery*
START / FINISH	*Grid reference: SO 224963*
DOG FRIENDLINESS	*Farming country – dogs should be on lead. Not allowed in castle grounds*
PARKING	*Car park on Bishops Castle Street on B4385 at south end of town*
PUBLIC TOILETS	*Behind town hall*

Montgomery is a fine country town with its origins in medieval times. Tucked beneath a castle-topped crag, many of the houses have Georgian façades, but these were additions to much older dwellings. The centrepieces of the town are the elegant red-brick town hall with a clock tower on top and the half-timbered Dragon Hotel, a 16th-century coaching house. Plaques on the walls of the old houses tell you of Montgomery's proud history, but you can learn more by calling into the Old Bell Inn, which has been converted into a museum.

Controlling the Welsh Marches

After William I conquered England in 1066 he gave the task of controlling the Welsh Marches to his friend and staunch supporter, Roger de Montgomery. Montgomery set up a motte-and-bailey timber castle at Hendomen a mile (1.6km) north of the present town.

Continuous Skirmishes

There were continuous skirmishes with the Welsh, especially with the coming to power of Llewelyn the Great, Prince of Wales. As a result, Henry III had the current castle built in 1223 on a huge rock overlooking the plains of the River Severn. In 1541 the new English monarch, Henry VII, a Welshman descended from Llewelyn, handed the castle to the Herberts, a powerful Welsh dynasty, who were later to acquire the neighbouring Powis Castle. The castle saw its last action during the Civil War. The Herberts were Royalists and at first held the castle, but in a great battle in which their 5,000 troops were attacked by 3,000 Parliamentarians, it was the Parliamentarians who were finally victorious. In 1649 they demolished the castle. When you view it today though, it's still an impressive place and you get this feeling of impregnability as you look down those tremendous cliffs.

The next castle you see on the walk though is much earlier. When emerging from the woods, the sight of the giant earthworks of Ffridd Faldwyn makes it obvious that this hilltop Iron Age fort was of great importance. It was built in four stages, all completed before the Roman conquest. Artefacts, including neolithic tools, are held in the National Museum of Wales in Cardiff.

Distant Views

After making a brief return to the outskirts of Montgomery the route undertakes one of the locals' favourite Sunday strolls – to the top of Town Hill, where the war memorial stands tall to commemorate the soldiers of the county. The Automobile Association erected a toposcope to help scan the horizon for the well-known hills of Pumlumon Fawr, Stiperstones, the Clun Hills and the Long Mynd. The Severn can be seen in plan, weaving through forest and field in a landscape as green as any in Ireland.

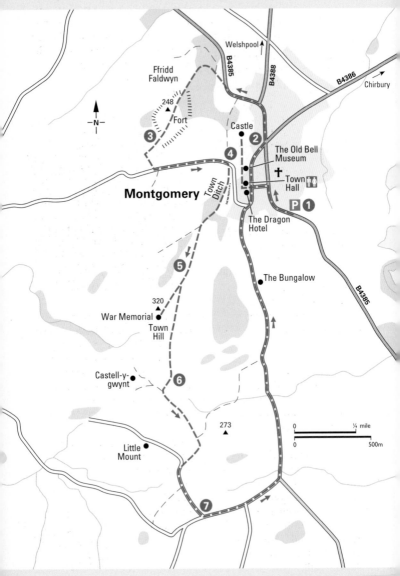

WALK 47 DIRECTIONS

1 From the car park head north, then left along Broad Street, where you'll see the town hall and The Dragon Hotel. A signpost to the castle points up the lane behind, the path then leaving right through a kissing gate. It's a must to see and is free. Return to this point. Head north up Arthur Street, past the Old Bell Museum.

WHERE TO EAT AND DRINK

The Dragon Hotel is an impressive and friendly old coaching inn. Here you can choose from an extensive menu with specials on a blackboard. Expect to find good local produce including Welsh lamb and beef, a wide choice for vegetarians, tasty pasta and game dishes. The beers include those from the local Wood brewery and Boddingtons.

2 Reaching the main road, go left and keep left with the B4385 in the direction of Newtown. Leave just past the speed derestriction sign, over a stile on the left. Bear right across a field towards trees. This path climbs through woodland, then swings left (south-west) to reach the old hilltop fort above Ffridd Faldwyn.

3 Over the stile at the far side of the fort, bear left downfield to the roadside gate. Turn left along the road, which takes you back towards Montgomery.

4 As the road turns sharp right just above the town, leave it for a footpath on the right signposted for the Montgomeryshire War Memorial and beginning beyond a kissing gate. The footpath climbs steadily up the hill to join a farm track, which at first runs parallel to the Town Ditch.

WHILE YOU'RE THERE

The Old Bell Museum gives a fascinating insight into the history of the town, its castles, workhouses and archaeological excavations. There is a room devoted to the Cambrian Railway.

5 As it enters high pastures, the track begins to level out and traverse the eastern hillside. Here you can make a detour to the war memorial that can be seen clearly ahead at the top of the hill. Return to the track and follow it through a gate and past some pens with gorse and hawthorn lining the way on the left.

WHAT TO LOOK OUT FOR

In 1279 Montgomery built new town walls of stone to protect itself from the attacks of Llewelyn the Great and, later, Dafydd ap Llewelyn. Not much remains of the walls themselves, but in places you'll see the Town Ditch that accompanied them. You can see the ditch alongside the track climbing to the war memorial and to the east of town behind the church.

6 Keep going in the next field, the hedge curving into the corner. Walk ahead through a wide gap and head downfield to leave by a gate and stile at the bottom. Follow a tarmac track down to a junction south-east of Little Mount farm and go left to a lane.

7 Keeping left at successive junctions, walk back to Montgomery. Turn right along Kerry Street into the square.

Remote Pumlumon's Corrie Lake

Discover Pumlumon's secret, a jewel of a tarn set among the rocks of the Rheidol's dark northern corrie.

DISTANCE 5.5 miles (8.8km) MINIMUM TIME 3hrs

ASCENT/GRADIENT 623ft (190m) ▲▲▲ LEVEL OF DIFFICULTY +++

PATHS Good track up, sketchy return path

LANDSCAPE Wild moorland

SUGGESTED MAP OS Explorer 213 Aberystwyth & Cwm Rheidol

START / FINISH Grid reference: SN 762861

DOG FRIENDLINESS Dogs are okay off lead outside summer months when sheep will be in lowland fields

PARKING Off-road parking – room for several cars by woods at start of walk, car park by Nant-y-moch dam

PUBLIC TOILETS Nearest at Ponterwyd

The phrase 'sodden weariness' has often been quoted by writers trying to describe Pumlumon and its environs. The description is unfair and used only by those who do not know the area very well. There are secrets to enjoying Pumlumon. Approach it from the north and you see the best of its crags and cwms, and you'll experience the feeling of remoteness. This lower-level route begins by the shores of Nant-y-moch Reservoir and sets out to discover an ice-scooped corrie reminiscent of those found in Northern Snowdonia.

Rescued from the Reservoirs

Nant-y-moch Reservoir was constructed in 1961. The water from the Nant-y-moch and Dinas reservoirs are pumped to the Rheidol hydro-electric power station to the south. Items rescued from a farm and chapel that were submerged by the lake can be seen at the visitor centre in Cwm Rheidol.

Hill of the Graves

Early on in the walk you pass beneath the rocks of Bryn y Beddau, a rather unremarkable piece of quarried moorland. But the name means hill of the graves, and therein lies a story. In 1401 the troops of Owain Glyndwr met those supporting the English King, Henry IV, on the northern slopes of Pumlumon. Glyndwr had only 400 men, the English had 1,500. The Welsh troops were hemmed in on all sides. The scene was set for the famous Battle of Nant Hyddgant. The Welshmen realised they would have to fight like fury or die. Many did both. They lost 200 fighters but in the process a famous victory was theirs. The battle gained Glyndwr a considerable following among his countrymen – one which would sweep him to power and help him to the title of Prince of Wales. The dead from the battle were buried here at Bryn y Beddau.

Dammed Tarn

Llyn Llygad Rheidol is a natural tarn, but unfortunately it was dammed and enlarged to supply water to Aberystwyth. Nevertheless this place still retains its beauty, especially on a day when the air is still and those crags reflect perfectly in glass-like waters.

Desolate Hyddgen Valley

On the return journey you'll be looking downstream and towards the Hyddgen Valley that stretches away to the north. Desolate and uninhabited these days, it is the site of a tragic tale of a shepherd who was caught in a violent blizzard. His wife was alarmed when his horse returned alone. She took a lamp, for it was now dark, and went in search. Eventually she found him unconscious and tried in vain to drag him back home but sadly both died on that ferocious night. It is said that at the end of each day a light can be seen, wavering as it travels from the valley to the spot where the shepherd fell.

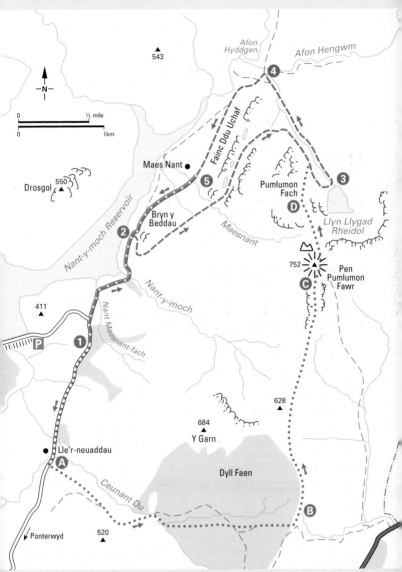

WALK 48 DIRECTIONS

1 From the car parking spaces beneath the woods east of the Nant-y-moch dam (near the spot height 392m on OS Explorer maps) walk north along the road and take the right-hand fork. The road descends to cross the streams of Nant Maesnant-fach and Nant-y-moch before traversing rough moorland along the east shores of Nant-y-moch Reservoir. The reservoir, stocked with native brown trout, is popular with anglers during the season.

WHILE YOU'RE THERE

Visit the Bwlch Nant-yr-Arian Forestry Centre just off the A44, west of Ponterwyd. Here you can learn about forestry and conservation with pictures and dioramas. Refreshments are available. You can watch the red kite feeding every day at 3pm (2pm winter). The centre is open 10am–5pm in summer and 10am–dusk in winter.

2 Beneath the quarried rocks of Bryn y Beddau, a rubble track on the right-hand side of the road doubles back up the hillside then swings round to the left. The steep sides of Pumlumon now soar away to the skyline on your right, with the little stream of Maesnant tumbling down them. Follow the track which climbs further, then levels out to pass some shallow lakes, which lie above the rocks of Fainc Ddu Uchaf. Now high above the bare valleys of the Hyddgen and Hengwm the track swings south beneath crags of Pumlumon Fach to arrive at Llyn Llygad Rheidol's dam.

3 To get to the footpath along the other side you'll have to ford the stream a short way downhill – take care if the stream is in spate.

The path, which runs parallel to the eastern banks of the stream, is sketchy in places, especially where you ford a side stream. It descends peaty terrain where mosses and moor grasses proliferate.

WHERE TO EAT AND DRINK

The Dyffryn Castell Hotel on the A44 just east of Ponterwyd is a 400-year-old whitewashed coaching inn set in the wilds of Wales and in the foothills of Pumlumon. It's family run and serves good home-cooked food in a bar, made cosy in winter by a glowing log fire.

4 When you reach a small stand of conifers in the Hengwm Valley, turn left to follow an old cart track which fords the Afon Rheidol, close to its confluence with the Afon Hengwm. The track heads west and soon the Hengwm Valley meets that of the Afon Hyddgen. The track swings to the south-west and passes between the squat cliffs of Fainc Ddu Uchaf and the western shores of Nant-y-moch Reservoir.

5 Go through the gate above the outdoor pursuits centre at Maes Nant and continue along the tarmac lane, joining in the outward route. Return to the car park and the start of the walk.

WHAT TO LOOK FOR

The red kite can often be seen flying here. They had become nearly extinct with only a few breeding pairs here in Central Wales, but these days are more widespread. Red kites have been imported from Spain to make up the numbers, and feeding centres have been set up to encourage the bird to stay in the area (See While You're There).

On Pumlumon Fawr

*Scan the horizon, from Cardigan Bay to
Snowdonia and Brecon.*
See map and information panel for Walk 48

DISTANCE 10 miles (16.1km)   **MINIMUM TIME** 6hrs
ASCENT/GRADIENT 1,640ft (500m) ▲▲▲   **LEVEL OF DIFFICULTY** +++
NOTE Very remote country, so save walk for good weather

WALK 49 DIRECTIONS
(Walk 48 option)

Pumlumon, which means five peaks, has historically been considered to be one of the three major mountains of Wales, along with Snowdon and Cadair Idris. Though it's not as spectacular as the other two, it's a noble mountain with views across the whole of Wales. On this walk start by heading south along the road from the parking area. Just past Lle'r-neuaddau farm, take the track on the left, Point **Ⓐ**, heading towards the forest of Dyll Faen.

Where the track enters the forest, turn right at a bridleway marker and follow the stream. The path is rough and wet on the ground, but it's a short section. Cross a side stream, turn left through a gate and enter the forest. Follow narrow grassy rides, with occasional waymarks, to a stile at the eastern edge.

Once out of the forest, turn left (Point **Ⓑ**) and follow a broad track to a gate, beyond which a clear footpath heads directly up the ridge to the trig point on Pen Pumlumon Fawr, Point **Ⓒ**.

The summit view is a memorable one. To the west, Nant-y-moch slips away into brown hills and inky forests, leading the eye to the thin blue line of Cardigan Bay. In the south the angular ridges of the Brecon Beacons, Black Mountains and Mynydd Ddu fill the view, while to the north Cadair Idris reigns.

Ignore the fence now and head north past a final cairn. (In thick mist it is safer to retrace the route of ascent.) The descent is steep and stony at first, but soon the gradients ease. The path all but gives up on Pumlumon Fach but the broad grassy ridge will take you safely down to the gravel track to the east. Join this as soon as you can see the easy slope down to the right (Point **Ⓓ**, no path). (If mist does come down keep north along the declining spur until you rejoin the main track. In these conditions it's better to return along this track, used in Walk 48 between Points **②** and **③**, and not the sketchy footpath back to Bryn y Beddau, between Points **③** and **④**.)

Providing it is clear, turn right along the track and follow it to the dam of Llyn Llygad Rheidol, Point **③**. From here you follow Walk 48 back to the start.

From Borth to Aberystwyth

A linear coastal walk from the Dyfi to the Ystwyth estuaries with some history on the way.

DISTANCE 6 miles (9.7km)   MINIMUM TIME 3hrs

ASCENT/GRADIENT 1,184ft (350m) ▲▲▲   LEVEL OF DIFFICULTY +++

PATHS Good coast path eroded in places, 4 stiles

LANDSCAPE Sea cliffs and promenades

SUGGESTED MAP OS Explorer 213 Aberystwyth & Cwm Rheidol,
tiny part on Explorer OL23 Cadair Idris & Llyn Tegid

START Grid reference: SN 608900 (just on Explorer OL23)

FINISH Grid reference: SN 586815

DOG FRIENDLINESS Can run free on coast path, but under close control

PARKING Car park at entrance to Borth village (free)
or round corner from Aberystwyth Station (pay)

PUBLIC TOILETS At Aberystwyth car park or on sea front at Borth

NOTE Regular train and bus service, except on Sundays

WALK 50 DIRECTIONS

Borth is a one-street town trying desperately, but not quite succeeding, to be a real seaside resort – it's dog-eared and not very pretty. Where Borth scores, however, is in its position. To the north, bordering the Dyfi Estuary, lies the peat bog of Cors Fochno, an important National Nature Reserve. To the south are sea cliffs with superb airy walks, the best of which is the linear walk to Aberystwyth.

Turn left from the station and follow the main street or grey shingle beach. Follow Cliff Road to its end where the cliff path begins, climbing past the war memorial. Looking back you can see Borth stretching out to the sands of the Dyfi Estuary. But the dominant feature of this view is Cors Fochno, a vast flat area of wetlands. Descend to a cove below the regimented

Pen-y-Graig caravan park before climbing back to the top of the cliffs. Always to the left you'll see a system of lush fields, while to the right there is often a bird's-eye view of the beach below.

There's another steep descent and re-ascent west of Brynbala Farm, which lies at the foot of a rounded coastal hill of the same name. The path traverses a steep slope before coming to a little valley inhabited by a huge house, Wallog. Descend to cross the stream and you will pass the seaward front of the house, then continue along the coast path.

Clarach Bay comes as a bit of a shock – a testament to bad taste and poor planning. A naturally beautiful green valley has been filled with caravans and chalets, with no trees to hide the glaring whiteness of their metal. Turn your eyes seawards and get through as quickly as possible.

ABERYSTWYTH

Cross a wooden bridge (the one elegant note hereabouts) and follow the road ahead until it bends left. Here, go right to follow a path that rakes through pinewoods. Clarach Bay disappears behind the hill and there are pathside seats, ideal for lunch or coffee-stops.

Suddenly you're back in the thick of it – on Constitution Hill. Many visitors arrive on the cliff railway, which was constructed in 1896. On the top there's a café, telescopes, a camera obscura and gift shop. Perhaps you can forgive Constitution Hill its commerciality, for it has a superb view of Aberystwyth and the Cardigan Bay coastline, from the Lleyn Peninsula in the north to Fishguard in the south.

After having a look around, continue on the coast path, which crosses then re-crosses the cliff railway before coming down to the town. Now follow the promenade, known as Marine Terrace. Here you see the sweep of Cardigan Bay framed by hundreds of Victorian terraced guest houses and a short pier jutting into the sea.

To dismiss Aberystwyth as a holiday resort would be to do it an injustice, for here is a town of great historical importance. Overlooking the harbour is the once mighty castle built in 1277 for Edward I as part of his impregnable 'iron ring'. During Edward's reign Welshmen were not allowed within the walls of the town, though with time and mixed marriages they soon were. The town and castle fell to the Welsh under Owain Glyndwr in 1404 and for a short time Wales had its Parliament here. With the demise of this last Welsh Prince of Wales however, the castle again became tangled up in English politics and fell victim to the Civil War. This led to its being blown up and left to disintegrate into the ruins you see today.

On Penparcau, the next hill, overlooking both the Rheidol and Ystwyth estuaries, are the earthwork remains of an Iron Age fort, which was probably founded around 600 BC. If your car is at Borth, then it will be too far for this itinerary, so head back to the railway station.

Walking in Safety

All these walks are suitable for any reasonably fit person, but less experienced walkers should try the easier walks first. Route finding is usually straightforward, but you will find that an Ordnance Survey map is a useful addition to the route maps and descriptions.

RISKS

Although each walk here has been researched with a view to minimising the risks to the walkers who follow its route, no walk in the countryside can be considered to be completely free from risk. Walking in the outdoors will always require a degree of common sense and judgement to ensure that it is as safe as possible.

- Be particularly careful on cliff paths and in upland terrain, where the consequences of a slip can be very serious.

- Remember to check tidal conditions before walking on the seashore.

- Some sections of route are by, or cross, busy roads. Take care and remember traffic is a danger even on minor country lanes.

- Be careful around farmyard machinery and livestock, especially if you have children with you.

- Be aware of the consequences of changes in the weather and check the forecast before you set out. Carry spare clothing and a torch if you are walking in the winter months. Remember the weather can change very quickly at any time of the year, and in moorland and heathland areas, mist and fog can make route finding much harder. Don't set out in these conditions unless you are confident of your navigation skills in poor visibility. In summer remember to take account of the heat and sun; wear a hat and carry spare water.

- On walks away from centres of population you should carry a whistle and survival bag. If you do have an accident requiring the emergency services, make a note of your position as accurately as possible and dial 999.

COUNTRYSIDE CODE

- Be safe, plan ahead and follow any signs.

- Leave gates and property as you find them.

- Protect plants and animals and take your litter home.

- Keep dogs under close control.

- Consider other people.

For more information visit www.countrysideaccess.gov.uk/things_to_know/countryside_code